MAKING & MEANING
THE WILTON DIPTYCH

Sponsored by Esso UK plc

MAKING & MEANING
THE WILTON DIPTYCH

Dillian Gordon

With an essay by Caroline M. Barron and contributions by Ashok Roy and Martin Wyld

NATIONAL GALLERY PUBLICATIONS, LONDON

This book was published to accompany an exhibition at
The National Gallery, London
15 September–12 December 1993

First published in Great Britain in 1993 by
National Gallery Publications Limited
5/6 Pall Mall East, London SW1Y 5BA

Reprinted 1993

ISBN 1 85709 036 5

525174

British Library Cataloguing-in-Publication Data.
A catalogue record for this book is available from the British
Library.

Editors: Diana Davies and Felicity Luard
Designed by Sally Jeffery

Printed and bound in Great Britain by
Butler and Tanner, Frome and London

Front cover: The Virgin and Child with Angels. Detail of the
interior of the right wing of the Wilton Diptych.
Back cover: The White Hart. Detail of the exterior of the left
wing.

CONTENTS

AUTHOR'S ACKNOWLEDGEMENTS

Friends and colleagues from a variety of disciplines have been unstintingly generous in responding to my queries, in offering advice and suggestions, and in sharing information. I am particularly grateful to Caroline Barron who has written the introductory essay, but I should also like to convey my deep thanks to all those devoted to research on Richard II and his court, and others who have each in some way contributed to this catalogue, namely Jonathan Alexander, Caroline Babington, Janet Backhouse, Paul Binski, Sarah Brown, Marian Campbell, John Cherry, Josephine Darrah, Caroline Elam, Celia Fisher, Julian Gardner, John Harvey, Martin Kauffmann, Maurice Keen, Ronald Lightbown, Richard Marks, Elly Miller, Shelagh Mitchell, Lisa Monnas, Richard Mortimer, David Park, Ann Payne, Olga Pujmanova, Christina Reast, Catherine Reynolds, Gervase Rosser, Lucy Freeman Sandler, Nigel Saul, Brian Spencer, Kay Staniland, Judith Stevenson, Dominique Thiébaut, Julia Walworth. I should also like to thank all my colleagues in the National Gallery who have worked so hard towards this exhibition and particularly Raymond White who analysed the medium samples of the diptych.

Dillian Gordon

SPONSOR'S PREFACE

We at Esso are privileged to sponsor this exhibition, the first in the 'Making and Meaning' series to be held at the National Gallery. As in previous partnerships between Esso and the National Gallery, it features not only works of art but excellent research and scholarship that are the Gallery's hallmarks. This exhibition illuminates the Wilton Diptych in a way that clarifies its meaning and helps the modern viewer to understand the influences that shaped it.

The diptych was meant for private devotion and admiration, so there is indeed pleasure to be had in having the opportunity to stand in front of it and appreciate both its scale and intensity through an intimacy with its images.

Offering the public the chance to enjoy a greater understanding of the Arts through access to exhibitions such as this lies at the very heart of the Arts sponsorship policy of Esso.

As sponsor of this exhibition Esso is delighted to continue its association with the National Gallery, a relationship which began with the 'Art in the Making' series. This exhibition maintains those high standards of excellence set then.

K. H. Taylor
Chairman and Chief Executive, Esso UK plc

FOREWORD

This exhibition is the first in a new series. It is sponsored by an old friend to the National Gallery. Some years ago, Esso UK plc supported a pioneering group of exhibitions, 'Art in the Making', which presented to a wide public the technical research of the Gallery's conservation and scientific departments. That success has encouraged us to embark on a second series, 'Making and Meaning', which will examine in detail one great painting from the Collection, looking both at how it was made and what it meant to those who saw it when it was new. There could be no better picture with which to start than the Wilton Diptych, the greatest painting to survive from fourteenth-century England, familiar to millions, yet puzzling in almost every aspect.

Richard II was in most ways a disastrous king. That he is today remembered far above more distinguished monarchs is due to no quality of his, but to his rare good fortune in being twice transmuted in a great work of art. We think of him now not as the unstable ruler he in fact was, but as the poetic martyr-victim of Shakespeare's play and the slender figure in the Wilton Diptych who kneels before his God.

The Wilton Diptych shows us Richard as he himself earnestly wanted to be: a king invested with supreme authority by Christ and the Virgin to whom he has committed his kingdom, a king surrounded by angels, sustained by the example and the intercessions of the three saints who played so large a part in his spiritual life – Edmund, Edward the Confessor and John the Baptist. It seems clear that the artist was also asked to show the king some years younger than he actually was, possibly in reference to his youthful accession to the throne. The Wilton Diptych in short shows us Richard as he saw himself and as he wanted his contemporaries to see him. To examine the very image of kingship that he chose to present is one of the purposes of this exhibition.

The other is to examine the Wilton Diptych itself. So few high-quality paintings survive from fourteenth-century England that the diptych has always seemed an isolated, puzzling phenomenon, just possibly an English work, more probably by a foreign artist working at the English court. Over the last two years it has been cleaned and carefully studied. Samples of the paint structure have been taken and analysed. The painting has above all been very carefully looked at. Surprisingly for such a well-known object, a great deal of new information about it has emerged and is published here. We can now be much clearer about how the artist achieved his effects and we can place him with more confidence in the context of the European art of his day. That art ranges far beyond other panel paintings, and the stature of the Wilton Diptych can perhaps now best be gauged as it is seen here, in the company of manuscript illuminations, stained glass, metal work and textiles.

It has been possible to bring these works of art together thanks only to great generosity on the part of the many lenders to the exhibition. We are extremely grateful to them for entrusting their objects to our care: we believe that a great deal will be learnt by having them here. Our greatest debt of gratitude – and it is an extraordinary one – is to our sponsors, Esso UK plc. Without their generosity and committed support, it would not have been possible either to mount such an exhibition, or to make it available to our public free of charge. To know more about the Wilton Diptych is to have more ways of enjoying it. It is also to be more aware than ever how ungraspable, how mysterious a work of art it remains.

Neil MacGregor
Director

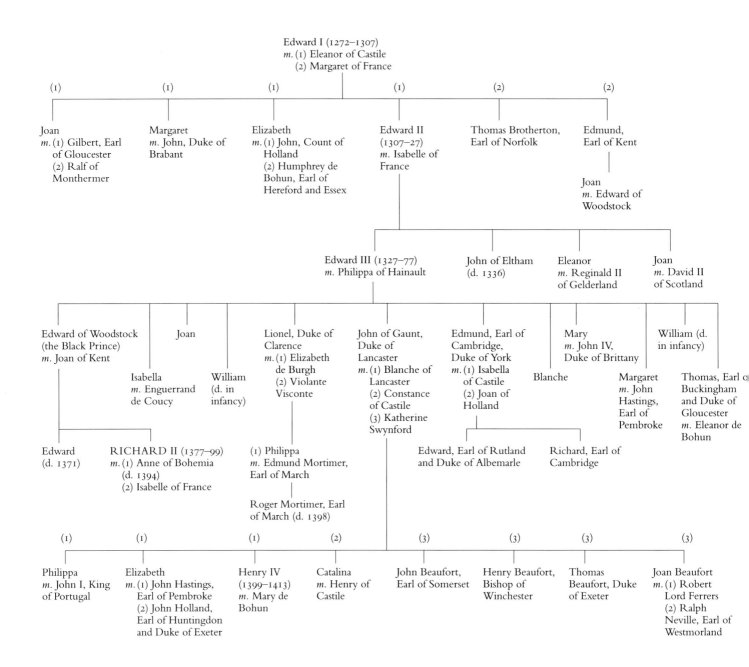

Introduction

The Wilton Diptych is so called because from the eighteenth century until it entered the National Gallery Collection in 1929 it was at Wilton House, the Wiltshire seat of the Earls of Pembroke. This small portable altarpiece, consisting of two hinged panels, painted on both sides (Plates 1–4), was almost certainly intended for the private religious devotions of Richard II, King of England from 1377 to 1399, and is one of the most beautiful paintings ever made. The intricacy of detail, the refinement and subtlety of its varied techniques and decorative effects, the richness of its colours and the tooling of the gold are unmatched in any surviving painting. Yet it has puzzled generations of scholars. No one knows who painted it, or why, or what it means.

The imagery could well have been drawn from the world of medieval myth and legend, from the Arthurian romances of Chrétien de Troyes or the tales of Marie de France: an arrow and a ring with magic properties; a beautiful Virgin holding a baby wrapped in a golden cloak and surrounded by curly-haired maidens standing in a meadow strewn with flowers; a young king in gorgeous apparel kneeling in a wasteland before a forest, accompanied by two other kings and a hermit dressed in animal skins; a white hart with golden antlers, a golden crown and a chain around its neck; a knight's shield and helm guarded by a golden lion – all these are the potential ingredients of a fairy-tale.

The historical reality behind the people whose story is linked to the Wilton Diptych is brutally different – a young man who had come to the throne of England aged ten, and had been widowed, married again, deposed and probably murdered by his cousin before he reached the age of thirty-three; another king who had intermittent bouts of madness, and whose brother was violently murdered by his own uncle; a child bride who at the age of seven was married to the king of England, widowed when she was ten, and who was later to marry one of France's greatest poets and die in childbirth aged nineteen. These three people – Richard II, King of England, Charles VI, King of France, and Isabelle, his daughter – are the key figures in the story of the Wilton Diptych.

At first glance the Wilton Diptych seems straight-forward. All the people shown can be identified: the kneeling king, Richard II, is being presented to the Virgin and Child by Saints John the Baptist, Edward the Confessor and Edmund. All the heraldic emblems are identifiable: around his neck the king wears a collar of pods of the broom plant (or broomcods), and at his breast a jewel of a white hart, well-known as his personal emblem. On the exterior of one wing, lying on a bank of flowers and foliage, including rosemary, is the white hart again, lodged or couchant, and gorged, while the exterior of the other wing has the royal arms of England and France ancient (lions passant guardant and fleurs-de-lis) impaled with the mythical arms of Edward the Confessor (a cross patonce between five martlets), a combination used by Richard. Above the royal arms is a helmet of silver leaf which has now largely disappeared and a red cap of maintenance with a white lining, now badly damaged, and above that a lion statant guardant. Originally they would have looked something like the arrangement of arms illustrated in the early fifteenth-century manuscript shown in Plates 27 and 28.

But nothing about the painting is unequivocal. Why is Richard shown with those particular saints? What does the gesture of his half-open hands mean – are they empty or praying? Why are the figures in the left wing in a wasteland, while the Virgin and Child and angels are in a flowery meadow? What exactly is the interaction between the figures in the left and right wings? What is the Child doing? He could be blessing the king, or be about to present the banner to him, or have just received the banner from him. What exactly is the nature of this banner? Why are there symbols of Christ's Passion drawn in the Child's halo? Why are the angels wearing collars and white harts similar to those of the king? What is the significance of their gestures towards the king? Is one intended to read the composition from left to right, or right to left, or both? Did Richard commission the diptych himself, and if so why? Or was it a gift? Or was it commissioned after his death?

Just as the imagery is straightforward and yet extremely complex, so are the technical features. The diptych is visibly a painting on panel with a gold background gilded in a traditional manner, with gold leaf laid over orange bole which now shows through in the damaged exterior panel. This gold background is exquisitely tooled, the pigments used demonstrably expensive, with lavish use of ultramarine for the blue robes.

However, detailed technical examination reveals that this is by no means a straightforward panel painting. The wood is oak and the ground is chalk as commonly used by North European painters. But the pigments have been bound with an egg medium, and the flesh tones undermodelled with green earth, a common practice among Italian panel painters. The cloth-of-gold robes, which are superficially similar, have been executed using two quite different methods. The gold background is profusely stippled, like that in European panel painting of the time, yet the way in which the painter has used the stippling to model three-dimensionally is without parallel. And who was the painter? There are no contemporary documents or comparable works which afford any clue.

Recently the diptych was cleaned and it was possible to examine it with scientific equipment and technology not previously available. The new information gleaned, together with as much of the related material as possible, will be presented in this book in an attempt to explore some of the questions and some of the answers which have been proposed. But the conclusions must be left to the reader.

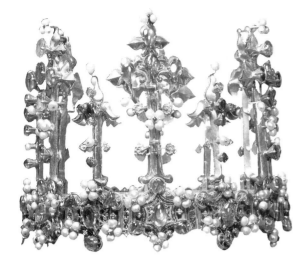

RICHARD II: IMAGE AND REALITY *Caroline M. Barron*

Not all the water in the rough rude sea
Can wash the balm off from an anointed king;
The breath of worldly men cannot depose
The deputy elected by the Lord[1]

The Richard II made famous by Shakespeare's play is portrayed as a flippant and irresponsible young man who cares little for his kingdom and less for the death of his uncle, 'time-honoured Lancaster'. Yet in the space of two years he is brought through adversity and the loss of kingly power to a position of moral supremacy and, ultimately, to a courageous death.[2] Although we know that in some repects he deserved his fate, by the end of the play our sympathies lie with Richard. What had happened that a young man who began his reign as a popular king should have reached the point where his magnates distrusted him to the extent of seeking his deposition?

Although Shakespeare's interpretation of the reign does not accord in every respect with that of modern historians, his portrait of Richard carries more conviction than some of his other medieval kings. Contemporary, or near-contemporary, chronicles seem to have been his main sources, but it is possible that he had also seen the Wilton Diptych. Several passages in the play are suggestive of the painting. John of Gaunt's description of England as

> . . . this little world,
> This precious stone set in the silver sea[3]

recalls the tiny map of a green island set in a sea of silver leaf recently discovered on the orb at the top of the banner in the right-hand panel of the diptych.

Moreover, the eleven angels who all clearly display their support for Richard by wearing the king's badge of the white hart, may have been in Shakespeare's mind when he wrote:

> God for his Richard hath in heavenly pay
> A glorious angel: then, if angels fight,
> Weak men must fall, for heaven still guards the right.[4]

Whatever his sources, Shakespeare used them to good effect to create a sympathetic and convincing figure. The king who emerges from the pen of the historian is not so greatly different from Shakespeare's character, but he is more prosaic perhaps and less sharply delineated. Here we have to set aside the dramatic hero of *Richard II* and the kneeling innocent of the Wilton Diptych, and search for the man who inspired both of these masterpieces.

Richard was born on 6 January 1367, the feast of the Epiphany, at Bordeaux where his father was on campaign. He was the second son of Edward the Black Prince and his wife Joan, 'the fair maid of Kent'. In fact Richard was Joan's seventh and last child, since she had three sons and two daughters by her first husband, Sir Thomas Holland. When he was four years old his elder brother, Edward of Angoulême, died and Richard was brought back to England in 1371. The Black Prince also returned to England, already stricken with the illness from which he was to die five years later at the age of forty-six. It is thus likely that Richard spent most of his time with his mother and also, perhaps, with his half-brothers and sisters. The influence of Princess Joan upon her son may be detected in Richard's later adoption of her

Fig. 1 (above) Crown thought to have belonged to Anne of Bohemia. French(?), *c.*1370–80. Gold set with sapphires, rubies and diamonds and decorated with enamelling, 18 cm high. Munich, Residenz, Schatzkammer.

badge of the white hart as his own particular badge. Edward the Black Prince predeceased his father, the old king Edward III, who continued to rule England for another year. On 22 June 1377, the eve of the Vigil of Saint John the Baptist, Richard succeeded his grandfather as king of England.

Richard was ten years old when he became king: old enough to understand the importance of the coronation, but not old enough to control events. Almost exactly fifty years earlier Richard's great-grandfather, Edward II, had been deposed and murdered. His son, under the influence of his mother, the French queen Isabelle, had acquiesced in his father's fate. He was fourteen at the time and may well have had little choice, but he seems to have been able to learn from his father's mistakes. When he was seventeen Edward III took control of the government and, by the happy combination of an affable nature and successful campaigns against the French, maintained harmony at home and united the nobility in exploits against the enemy on foreign soil. Richard, therefore, succeeded a very popular king, which made his own task harder. But his political inheritance was not an easy one: since 1369 the war against the French had become increasingly expensive and unsuccessful; there were rivalries among Edward's surviving sons, and, after the death in 1369 of his queen, Philippa of Hainault, the role played by the king's mistress, Alice Perrers, fomented jealousy and disharmony at court.

While Richard was considered to be too young to rule in person, the business of the realm was conducted by a minority council composed of men drawn from a wide spectrum of noble factions. But there could be little doubt that the real power behind the throne was John of Gaunt, Duke of Lancaster and, by right of his wife, King of Castile. He was Richard's eldest surviving uncle and, after the king, the richest and most powerful man in England. Richard himself seems to have maintained a low profile, living with his mother and the remnants of the Black Prince's household at the royal palaces of Eltham, Sheen or Windsor. Sir Guichard d'Angle (created Earl of Huntingdon at Richard's coronation), veteran of the wars in France, was appointed as Richard's 'governor', and it may have been from him that Richard learnt the French which so impressed the French chronicler and poet Froissart when he came to visit the king in the 1390s. That Richard spoke and read French very well is, perhaps, surprising when one remembers that after his return from Bordeaux in 1371 he never crossed the Channel again except for his brief trip to Calais in 1396 to marry his second wife, the French princess Isabelle. When Guichard

d'Angle died in 1380, Sir Simon Burley succeeded him as Richard's tutor. He too had fought with the Black Prince in France and an inventory of his library drawn up before his death shows that he owned a considerable number of French books, including romances, religious works and a French translation of the Bible.[5] So Richard's education in French culture would have continued. It may have been this which, in part, led Richard to support a policy of peace with France. As a corollary to this he developed a concept of kingship which emphasised the priestly rather than the military aspects. As the Wilton Diptych demonstrates, Richard came to identify himself not with the popular nationalistic Saint George who was thought to support the English against the French, but rather with the sainted Edward the Confessor who, by his diplomacy, defended England from invasion and developed a reputation less for manly prowess than for piety and wisdom.

In the country at large the ravages of the Black Death (1348–9 and 1361) had led to a scarcity of labour which encouraged working men and women to demand, and often to secure, greater personal freedom, higher wages and greater social mobility. Arable land was turned over to pasture, since there were fewer mouths to feed, and cattle were reared for their milk and for meat, and sheep for their wool, which was increasingly being manufactured into cloth. In Oxford, John Wycliffe was developing ideas which challenged the teachings of the Church about the priesthood, the sacrament of the Mass, the cult of saints and the doctrine of purgatory. Most importantly, Wycliffe urged that the Bible should be translated into English so that all men might have access to the Scriptures. Wycliffe's challenge to the Church did not go unanswered: among the defenders was Roger Dymok, a prominent Dominican friar who wrote a book refuting Wycliffe's heresies and presented it to Richard in 1395 (see Plate 11). Dymok wrote his book in Latin but throughout England, quite suddenly, English was becoming the language not only of the working man but also of business, in the law courts, in literature and at court. By the time of Richard's accession, Geoffrey Chaucer, an esquire of the Royal Household, had already written *The Book of the Duchess*, his translation of Boethius and *The House of Fame*. In London, William Langland was actively composing his life's work, the great alliterative poem *Piers Plowman*. It was a season of experiment and opportunity, of rising expectations and rising standards of living.

Richard's reign may be clearly divided into two periods: the years 1377 to 1388 and the years 1389 to

1399. Each culminated in a crisis which not only threatened Richard personally but also challenged the monarchy. The crisis of the years 1386 to 1388 jolted Richard into maturity and led him to take his kingship seriously. In the second period he worked to restore, as he saw it, the prerogatives of the monarchy. It is to this later period that the Wilton Diptych belongs. The painting is a tangible and visible witness to Richard's renewed interest in his particular and special role as king of England. But, unfortunately for Richard, although kings may be made in heaven, they have to fashion their own success on earth, and Richard failed not once, but twice.

When Richard was fourteen, the political incompetence of the minority councils, the unpopularity of John of Gaunt, the novelty and injustices of the poll-taxes of 1377, 1379 and 1380, and the upward mobility of the peasantry, combined to provoke the mass protest known as the Peasants' Revolt, although many townspeople and poorer clergy were also involved. The inadequacies of the government were laid bare by the events of June 1381 when the king and his councillors were, effectively, besieged in the Tower of London. Twice Richard rode out to meet the rebels, and although they professed loyalty to him and demanded only the execution of the 'traitors' around him the journeys must have been a considerable test of Richard's courage. Before confronting the rebels at Smithfield on 15 June, Richard went first to Westminster Abbey to pray at the Confessor's shrine, and he may well have attributed his subsequent success in dispersing the rebels to the intervention of the saint. There is no doubt that Richard held Westminster Abbey and its saint, Edward the Confessor, in particular veneration, as the diptych bears witness.[6] At Smithfield the rebel leader, Wat Tyler, was wounded in an altercation (possibly deliberately provoked) with those around the king. When Tyler's followers saw that he was wounded, they drew their bows ready to avenge his death. At this critical juncture Richard 'with marvellous presence of mind and courage for so young a man' rode towards the commons and said, 'What is this, my men? What are you doing? Surely you do not wish to fire on your own king? . . . I will be your king, your captain and your leader. Follow me into the field where you can have all the things that you would like to ask for.[7] Doubtless the contemporary chroniclers embroidered the story, but it seems certain that Richard, with a combination of courage, political sense and luck, said and did the right thing at a moment of crisis and thereby prevented a great deal of bloodshed. It probably confirmed his veneration for Saint Edward and it may

have led him to become unduly confident about his own powers and his invulnerablility. He would have been a young man of remarkable character and maturity if he had not had his head turned, first by an elaborate coronation when he was ten, and then by a near-miraculous exercise of charismatic leadership when he was fourteen.

Within a year Richard married Anne, the daughter of the Emperor Charles IV, King of Bohemia. The king's counsellors hoped by this marriage (for which no dowry was paid) to secure a place for England in the developing alliance of those who favoured Pope Urban VI against the anti-pope who was supported by the French and their allies. The marriage seems to have been a 'companionate' one: Richard and his new queen were almost exactly the same age and it would appear that they were happy together. There are no recorded infidelities on either side, but there were no children either. Here again Richard may have deliberately imitated the childless marriage of Edward the Confessor with Edith, the daughter of Earl Godwin. Was Richard, perhaps, striving for chastity within marriage? There is evidence that Richard was fond of his wife: they travelled around England together[8] and she was accorded a role in the formal ceremonies at Westminster Abbey on Saint Edward's feast day.[9] When Anne died in 1394 Richard gave vent to his rage and grief by ordering that the manor of Sheen where she had died should be utterly demolished.[10] He personally chose the designs for the copper-gilt effigies (Fig. 2) for their joint tomb chest near the Confessor's tomb at Westminster. Their epitaph records that Anne was 'corpore formosa vultu mitis speciosa' (gentle, with a beautiful body and a gracious face). She was the first English queen to share a tomb with her husband, and it was Richard's decision to show himself holding her hand.[11]

Until her death in 1385 Richard's mother, Joan of Kent, may well have continued to influence her son, but Anne was also a gentle presence in the background. At this time Robert de Vere, the young Earl of Oxford, was prominent at Richard's court and his promotion to the rank of Marquis of Dublin and then Duke of Ireland provoked jealousy among the magnates. But in the 1380s Richard was either unwilling or unable to take seriously the duties of kingship. He displayed the swift changes of mood characteristic of adolescents: in 1383 he suddenly decided to lead a rescue force across the Channel to salvage the disastrous expedition to Flanders led by Bishop Despenser of Norwich, but then equally suddenly abandoned the idea. He reacted angrily when John of Gaunt attempted to influence the decisions of the Council

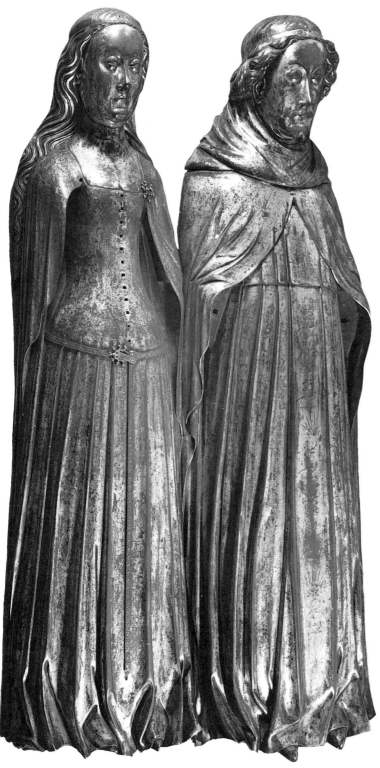

Fig. 2 Effigies of Richard II and Anne of Bohemia from their joint tomb in Westminster Abbey, commissioned 1395. Copper gilt.

and he quarrelled openly with him when they led a joint expedition to Scotland in 1385. On one occasion he nearly ran his sword through the Archbishop of Canterbury when he said something that annoyed him. It was the aim of Richard's Council, headed by the Chancellor, Michael de la Pole, Earl of Suffolk, to pursue a policy of peace with France. Richard seems to have supported this policy, but it was by no means universally popular. Many who could remember the great victories of Edward III's reign, and others like Richard's youngest uncle, Thomas of Woodstock, who had been too young to win fame and fortune in those happy days, grumbled at the failure to wage war successfully against the French. It was also thought that Richard's household was unnecessarily expensive: in fact the annual expenditure of the King's Wardrobe in the 1380s was not particularly high, but creditors were having to wait a very long time before they were paid.[12] Moreover, the young men whom Richard recruited as his chamber knights were regarded as upstarts, 'more potent in the bedchamber than on the battlefield, stronger with the tongue than with the lance'.[13]

As Richard's popularity waned, the fate of Edward II rose to the surface of men's minds. When Parliament was summoned in the autumn of 1386, Richard refused to attend and remained at Eltham. The assembled members sent Thomas of Woodstock, now Duke of Gloucester, and Thomas Arundel, Bishop of Ely, on a deputation to the king urging him to come to Parliament to pursue the war with France. If he did not attend to the business of the kingdom then the people might legitimately depose him. Richard came to Parliament. There he was forced to preside over the impeachment of his Chancellor, Michael de la Pole, and to see his government put into the hands of fourteen commissioners for a year. Richard's response was to spend the year away from London travelling around his kingdom so that he could avoid submitting publicly to the control of the commissioners. As the year came to an end, Richard took the advice of his judges as to the legality of Parliament's actions in impeaching the king's ministers without his consent, imposing on him a commission and in other ways curtailing his freedom of action. How should they be punished who threatened the king with the fate of Edward II? The response of the judges (who may have been coerced, although this is by no means certain) was that those who did such things should be punished as traitors.

Not surprisingly, when news of the judges' response was 'leaked' to those who had supported the commission, they quickly took action to retaliate.

Five lords, known as the Appellants, led by Thomas, Duke of Gloucester, and Richard, Earl of Arundel, accused five of Richard's close supporters of treason, including Michael de la Pole and Robert de Vere. Richard accepted the appeals (charges) of treason and agreed that they should be heard in the high court of Parliament, summoned to meet in February 1388. Meanwhile, in a costly error of judgement, he allowed Robert de Vere to 'escape' from custody and to ride to Chester to raise the king's men, those who were retained as his knights and esquires, in an attempt to destroy the five Appellants in advance of the meeting of Parliament. But the attempted *coup* was a failure: de Vere lost control of his men in the December fog at Radcot Bridge on the Thames, and the hastily summoned retinues of the five Appellants marched on London, newly emboldened with righteous indignation.

Richard had played a risky hand and lost: he was now revealed as untrustworthy for he had allowed de Vere to escape, and he had tried to use his own men against his 'loyal' subjects. The spectre of deposition moved closer. Holed up in the Tower of London, with the triumphant Appellants and their retinues controlling the city, Richard must have been reminded of the dangerous days of June 1381. For two or three days at the end of December 1387 Richard may actually have been deprived of royal authority, in effect briefly deposed. What saved him in this crisis was the division between his opponents. In particular Richard's cousin, Henry of Derby, the son of John of Gaunt (who was absent in Spain pursuing his own dynastic interests, but whose presence might well have prevented such a rebellion against Richard), saw no reason why Thomas, Duke of Gloucester, his father's youngest brother, should become king. In their rivalry lay Richard's salvation. But the meeting of Parliament, later known as the Merciless Parliament, lay ahead. Richard had no cards left to play. He sat by helplessly while five of his closest advisers were found guilty of treason (for giving the king unpopular advice deemed to be in their own interests rather than that of the realm) and the two who had not already escaped abroad were executed. Four of Richard's chamber knights were also executed, including Sir Simon Burley, his old tutor, for whom Queen Anne pleaded on her knees to Gloucester. The judges who had supported Richard's view of royal authority by their answers to his questions put to them in the previous summer, barely escaped with their lives. Two dozen lords and ladies were expelled from Richard's court and his household was, temporarily, destroyed as a social unit. The five Appellant lords had used Parliament to attack the king's ministers and friends when they could not attack the king himself. Before this vengeful Parliament finally dispersed in June, the king was present at a Solemn Mass at Westminster Abbey. Richard sat on a throne in front of the high altar and before him was placed a book and a cross. Here, in the Abbey and within the protection of the Confessor, 'he renewed the oath which he had taken at his coronation', and the lords spiritual and temporal also renewed the oaths which bound them in allegiance to their king.[14] Richard then thanked the lords and gave them leave to return home. The king had been forced to preside over a meeting of Parliament which had witnessed the nadir of royal authority. He had been unable to control events or to save his friends; he and his queen had been publicly humiliated; and he had been brought face to face with the limitations of royal power.

The years 1386–8 thus mark a watershed in Richard's kingship: his adolescent flippancy was now replaced by a new seriousness. In May 1389 he summoned a meeting of the Great Council to Westminster and declared that since he had reached an age of maturity (he was twenty-one) he was going to cast off the control of others and 'to the exclusion of all negligence, with God's help to work tirelessly for the future, at the well-being and profit of my people and kingdom.'[15] There was no doubt about the seriousness with which he now pursued the business of government. In 1394 (and again in 1399) Richard led an expedition to Ireland to bring its 'wild chieftains' under control: the first English king to visit Ireland for nearly two hundred years. At home he brought the turbulent city of London to heel, curbed the endemic rioting there, fined the inhabitants £30,000 and compelled them to lay on a magnificent 'triumph' for himself and his queen to mark the city's reconciliation with its 'good lord'. In the north the virtually autonomous role of the earls of Northumberland was curtailed and royal servants were appointed in the localities as sheriffs and customs collectors. The loyalties of Cheshiremen, once focused upon the Black Prince, were now directed towards Richard himself and those who were retained for the king's service were given his badge of the white hart. A new court party was developed: the two younger Appellants, Henry Bolingbroke, Earl of Derby, and Thomas Mowbray, Duke of Norfolk, were won over to the king's cause, and the three older men were politically isolated and finally brought low in 1397 when Gloucester died at Calais (probably murdered on Richard's orders) and Arundel and Warwick were condemned as traitors.

Anne of Bohemia died in 1394 and, as part of his

policy of ending the war with France and securing a permanent peace, Richard agreed to marry Isabelle, the seven-year-old daughter of the French king. It is possible that after Anne's death Richard intended not to remarry, but to remain wedded to the memory of his dead queen. He may also have intended to be joined in spirit with his saintly predecessor, Edward the Confessor, hence the use on the Wilton Diptych, and elsewhere, of Richard's arms impaling those of the Confessor, as if they were husband and wife. To achieve the twenty-eight-year truce with France it was politic for Richard to marry Isabelle, but as she was only seven Richard would have been unable to consummate the marriage for at least another five years. This may well have suited him. Richard appears to have been quite unconcerned about his lack of an heir and, in general, more interested in his ancestors than in his descendants. Throughout the 1390s Richard worked to try to secure the canonisation of his deposed great-grandfather, Edward II. In 1390 he visited Gloucester where Edward was buried and it may have been then that he had his own badge of the white hart painted around the columns which flanked Edward's tomb.[16] The Exchequer records bear witness to the considerable sums which Richard spent in pursuing the canonisation at the Papal Curia and in 1395 two Italians were entrusted with the task of taking two gold cups, a gold ring set with a ruby and a 'Book of Miracles of Edward, late king of England, whose body was buried in the town of Gloucester', to Pope Urban.[17]

Richard's policy of peace with France made him less dependent upon Parliament, for his need for money was less acute. There was a striking rise in wardrobe expenditure in the 1390s, reaching nearly £38,000 in 1397.[18] Much of this money was used by Richard to create a court which was among the most refined in Europe. Its sophistication was nurtured by frequent contact with the culture of other European courts: members of Richard's household such as Geoffrey Chaucer, or Sir John Clanvow (author of *The Book of Cupid*), travelled on embassies to Italy and to France. Frenchmen, such as Froissart himself, or the verse chronicler Jean Creton visited the English court in the 1390s. The French writer Christine de Pisan (see Plate 12) admired the poetry of John Montagu, Earl of Salisbury, who had been one of Richard's chamber knights, and sent her son Jean to be brought up in his household. John Gower wrote his *Confessio Amantis* at Richard's request, and it has been argued that *Sir Gawain and the Green Knight* was composed to entertain the royal household as it travelled around the north-west of England.[19]

The royal court was also the scene of tournaments, religious festivals, musical entertainment and feasting. Richard appreciated good food, personal comfort and luxury. When he remodelled Eltham Palace he added a bath house as well as a room for dancing.[20] He spent great sums of money on clothes: when he met Charles VI for three days at Ardres in 1396 to complete the marriage negotiations, it was noted that Richard changed his attire three times, whereas the French king wore the same clothes throughout.[21] The inventory of Richard's possessions taken after his deposition bears witness to the visual splendour of his court.[22] It records rich robes such as those he is seen wearing in the Wilton Diptych, luxurious furs, plate gilded and patterned with all manner of flora and fauna, including Richard's badge of the white hart, and jewellery of all kinds – collars, rings and girdles richly embroidered and decorated with symbols of loyalty, lordship and love. Richard paid artists, writers and craftsmen to create for him an environment which was beautiful, pleasing and comfortable. But he was trying also to obliterate what had happened to him in 1386–8; to buy men to defend him and magnificent accessories to create the image of unassailable monarchy. Books and paintings were commissioned to express the sacral nature of his kingship. Bishops and clerks were also recruited to support and defend this spiritual view: men like Thomas Merks, Bishop of Carlisle, William Colchester, Abbot of Westminster, and a group of younger Cambridge graduates. There is some evidence that the king was interested in the theoretical side of kingship. He commissioned a work concerned with the influence of the planets on human affairs.[23] It was in astrology and in the mystical and priestly nature of kingship, rather than in an empirical analysis of what had gone wrong in 1387–8, that Richard sought a solution to the problems he faced.

In the end all Richard's efforts to strengthen the monarchy and to raise it above faction and, thereby, nearer to God, came to nothing. In the summer of 1399 the king was deposed by his cousin Henry, Earl of Derby, who seized the Crown. Richard had no heirs to succeed him and his reign was barren in many ways. But this deposed and unsuccessful king has left three portraits of himself: the majestic painting in Westminster Abbey, the Wilton Diptych and the fine and distinctive copper-gilt effigy on his tomb. There is no doubting the individuality of his appearance in all these portraits: the long nose, the mass of wavy red-gold hair, the heavy-lidded eyes and the finely arched eyebrows. Richard's mother was widely acclaimed as fair, and Richard seems also to have been a handsome man whose visual appearance was striking. A monk from Evesham Abbey wrote that Richard was of average height, with golden hair and a face which was pale, rounded and somewhat feminine. He flushed easily and spoke little with a slight stammer.[24]

The epitaph on his tomb, which we may presume Richard himself commissioned, is written in Latin hexameters. Here Richard is commemorated as pure, strong in body and wise as Homer. He favoured the Church, but trampled on the upstarts, destroyed heretics and their supporters and laid low those who violated 'regalia', that is the royal prerogatives. He asked Christ and John the Baptist to intercede for him with their prayers.[25] The Latin word 'regalia' describes both the physical and the intangible attributes of royalty. It was Richard's greatest mistake that he consistently mistook the golden regalia of kingship for the reality of royal power. In deposing Richard his nobles rejected not only Richard himself but also the sacral kingship which he had struggled so hard to promote. But while the ideals that inspired the Wilton Diptych are now almost entirely discarded, the painting itself remains as a cryptic and beautiful monument to the king who nurtured those ideals.

NOTES

1. William Shakespeare, *Richard II*, act III, scene 2, lines 54–7.
2. I am grateful to Dr Nigel Saul who kindly read an earlier draft of this essay and made a number of helpful suggestions. Dr Saul is currently writing the definitive biography of Richard II to be published by Eyre and Spottiswood in 1994.
3. Act II, scene 1, lines 45–6.
4. Act III, scene 2, lines 60–3.
5. See Clarke 1931 (reprinted, Oxford 1937, pp.120–1).
6. See Saul 1994 (in press) and *The Westminster Chronicle*, pp.8–10.
7. Thomas Walsingham's account translated in *The Peasants' Revolt of 1381* (ed. R.B. Dobson, 2nd ed. London 1983, p.179). See also the accounts of the author of the Anonimalle Chronicle and Froissart (Dobson, op. cit., pp.166 and 194–8).
8. *The Westminster Chronicle*, p.87.
9. *The Westminster Chronicle*, p.451.
10. H. Colvin, *History of the King's Works*, vol. II, London 1963, p.998; *Chronicon Adae de Usk 1377–1421* (ed. E.M. Thompson), London 1904, p.9.
11. Colvin, op. cit., vol. 1,1963, pp.487–8.
12. Given-Wilson 1986, p.139 and Appendix I.
13. Given-Wilson, op. cit., p.163.
14. *The Westminster Chronicle*, pp.295, 343.
15. *The Westminster Chronicle*, p.393.
16. *The Westminster Chronicle*, pp.437–9.
17. Around 1389 Richard wrote to the pope to press for Edward's canonisation, Perroy 1933, pp.62–3; Devon 1837, pp.259, 264.
18. Given-Wilson, op. cit., p.271.
19. Bennett 1992, pp.3–20, esp. pp.12–15.
20. Mathew 1968, p.32.
21. Meyer 1881, pp.212ff.
22. Palgrave 1836, III, pp.313–58.
23. Taylor, *Proceedings of the Leeds Philosophical and Literary Society*, 1971, pp.189–205, esp. pp.194–5.
24. Stow 1977, p.166.
25. For the text of the epitaph see *Royal Commission on Historical Monuments*, 1924, p.31.

FURTHER READING

F.R.H. Du Boulay and C.M. Barron (eds.), *The Reign of Richard II. Essays in honour of May McKisack*, London 1971.
C. Given-Wilson, *The Royal Household and the King's Affinity: Service Politics and Finance in England 1360–1413*, London 1986.
A. Goodman, *John of Gaunt: the Exercise of Princely Power in Fourteenth-Century Europe*, London 1992.
R.F. Green, *Poets and Princepleasers: Literature and the English Court in the Late Middle Ages*, Toronto 1980.
B. Hanawalt (ed.), *Chaucer's England: Literature in Historical Context*, Minneapolis 1992.
G. Mathew, *The Court of Richard II*, London 1968.
J.J.N. Palmer, *England, France and Christendom*, London 1972.
V.J. Scattergood and J.W. Sherborne (eds.), *English Court Culture in the Late Middle Ages*, London 1983.
A. Steel, *Richard II*, Cambridge 1941.
P. Strohm, *Social Chaucer*, London 1989.
A. Tuck, *Richard II and the English Nobility*, London 1973.

THE MEANING OF THE WILTON DIPTYCH

The Wilton Diptych as a Religious Image

The underlying meaning of the Wilton Diptych is tantalisingly cryptic: the individual elements of its imagery have many strands which can be teased out to form a complex web of allusions operating on both a secular and a religious level. This would not have seemed strange in the Middle Ages when secular and religious themes were not mutually exclusive but inextricably linked. Human life and politics were inseparable from a view of mankind as part of a scheme of Christian salvation.

Although the jewel-like appearance of the diptych places it in the category of a courtly luxury object to be treasured by the king together with his jewels and golden robes, its function first and foremost was a religious one. Its physical nature is essentially that of a portable altarpiece which could be closed like a book and set up on the altars of different churches and chapels. It was intended for private religious devotion, but this is not immediately apparent from the images on the exterior, which are uncompromisingly secular. Painted on the side which is uppermost when the diptych is closed is Richard's personal emblem of the white hart lying on a bank of foliage among branches of rosemary (Plate 1). Rosemary was one of the emblems of Richard's first wife, Anne of Bohemia, but seems to have become one of the royal emblems taken over by Richard as his own.[1] Painted on the other exterior side is another set of heraldic emblems personal to Richard (Plates 4 and 5): at the top a lion statant guardant and below the red cap of maintenance and silver helmet and the royal arms of England and France ancient (lions and lilies), which around 1395 Richard II had impaled with the mythical arms of Edward the Confessor (a cross patonce with martlets). Both exterior paintings are therefore entirely personal to Richard II, and when the diptych is closed the heraldic nature of the wings, signalling ownership, offers no clue as to what one may expect to find painted on the inside. But inside (Plates 2 and 3), the Wilton Diptych is ostensibly a religious painting. King Richard is being presented by three saints to the Virgin and Child surrounded by angels, one of whom carries a white banner with a red cross of the type normally carried by Christ in scenes of the Resurrection. Incised within the Child's halo are a crown

of thorns and three nails, symbols of Christ's Passion (Plates 20 and 35). The Child's movement is a complex fusion of gestures, but it seems incontrovertible that one of them involves blessing the king.

The Virgin and Child stand in a meadow strewn with flowers (Plate 22), contrasting with the rocky wasteland of the other panel, and evidently symbolising heaven. The only flowers certainly identifiable seem frequently to have had a religious significance: roses, strewn over the meadow and also worn as chaplets by the angels, refer to the purity of the Virgin;[2] the blue flowers appear to be violets, symbols of the humility of the Virgin,[3] or perhaps irises, referring to her sorrows.[4] Other plants include daisies, a blue periwinkle, ferns, clover and possibly small mushrooms in the bottom right-hand corner. It seems therefore legitimate to interpret the composition of the diptych as reading from left to right: the king will eventually be transferred from the wasteland in which he kneels to the flowery meadow, having been redeemed by Christ's Passion and Resurrection.

The Virgin was of course widely venerated in medieval Europe, and devotion to her on the part of the king would not have been unusual. Like most collections of rich patrons, the royal collection inventoried in 1400 after Richard's death contained a number of images of the Virgin.[5] Richard is said to have dedicated himself to the Virgin before a statue of her in a chapel in Westminster, possibly that of St Mary de la Pew in Westminster Palace or the chapel with the same name in Westminster Abbey, before riding out to confront Wat Tyler in the Peasants' Revolt in 1381. In 1383 he made a pilgrimage to Our Lady of Walsingham, travelling via Bury St Edmunds,[6] and in 1385 he ordered special robes embroidered with white harts in pearls for the feast of the Purification of the Virgin.

It was quite common in northern Europe for rulers to be portrayed kneeling in front of the Virgin and on the same scale (in Italy donor figures tended to be diminutive), and there is nothing exceptional in representing King Richard kneeling before the Virgin and Child in the Wilton Diptych – an image before which Richard would himself have knelt in prayer.

The Wilton Diptych as an Icon of Kingship

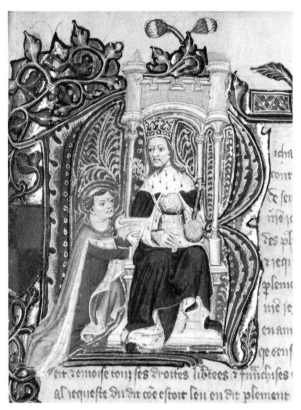

Fig. 3 Illuminated initial R showing Richard II receiving a presentation copy of the *Book of Statutes* (*Statuta Angliae*), after 1388, before 1399. Cambridge, St John's College, MS A 7, f.133.

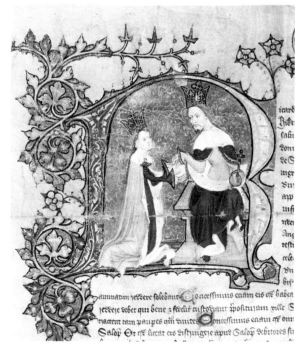

Fig. 4 Illuminated initial R showing Richard II and Anne of Bohemia. *Charter of Richard II to Shrewsbury*, 1389. Shrewsbury Museums, MS 1.24.

The Boy King

Having established the primary religious significance of the diptych, one is immediately faced with an anomaly. For it is not the Virgin, nor even the Child, but the king (Plate 6) who is the central focus of the composition of both wings. Every figure, with the exception of one angel, either gestures or looks towards him: the three saints behind him introduce him with their hands, while looking purposefully towards the Virgin and Child and the circle of eleven angels, who are all turned towards the king. Even the pointing finger of the angel at the extreme right was altered from its position in the initial design (see Fig. 29) to point not upwards at the Virgin and Child but unequivocally towards Richard: every detail ensures that the viewer looks first, not at the Virgin and Child, but at the kneeling king.

Richard's appearance in the diptych accords well with a description in a contemporary chronicle where he is said to be of common stature, his hair yellowish, his face fair, round and feminine and often flushed.[7] However, his portrait is one of the most puzzling features in this enigmatic painting. For it can be argued on the grounds of heraldry – namely the inclusion of the royal arms impaled with those of Edward the Confessor, and the inclusion of the broomcod motif – that the diptych was probably painted around 1396–7, and certainly no earlier than 1395. In 1395 Richard was already twenty-eight years old and yet in the diptych he appears much younger. Moreover, it is virtually certain that by this date he had a beard and moustache: it has been argued that he was bearded from at least 1388–9 (see for example Figs. 3 and 4). There are approximately twenty surviving representations of him in manuscripts and sculpture but they provide unreliable records of his appearance at any particular date, largely because the portraitists seem to have used patterns rather than studies from life.[8] But in his tomb effigy (Figs. 5 and 6) in Westminster Abbey we have a record of his appearance in 1395 which is likely to be reliable, for the contract drawn up in April 1395 specifies that the king is to be portrayed according to a pattern shown to the coppersmiths,[9] and this

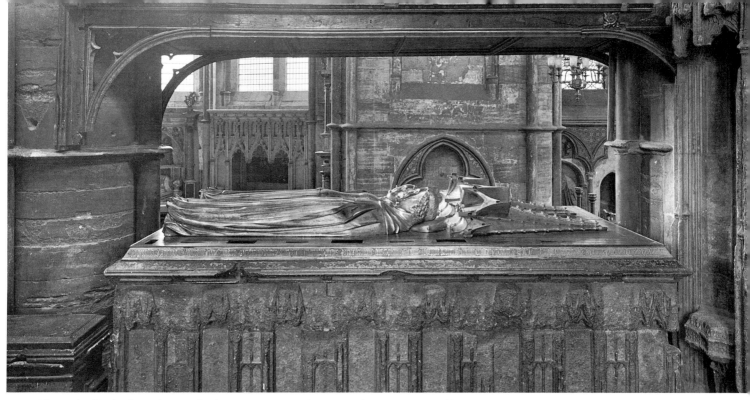

Fig. 5 The tomb of Richard II and Anne of Bohemia, commissioned 1395. London, Westminster Abbey.

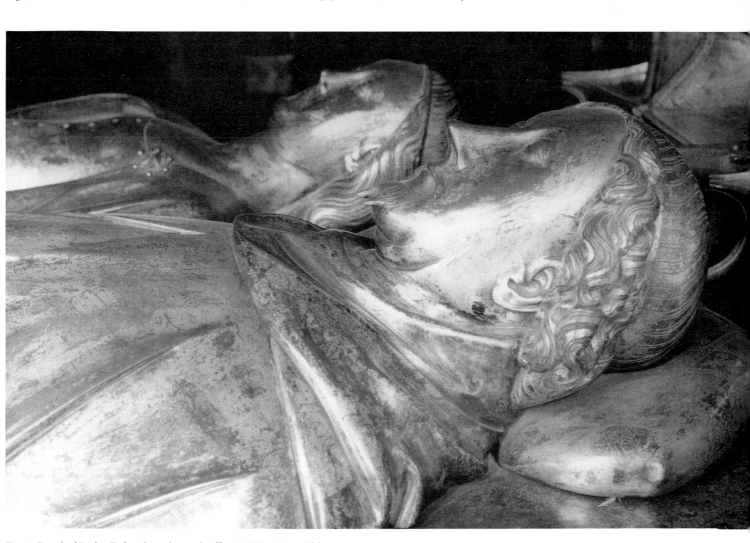

Fig. 6 Detail of Richard's face from the tomb effigy in Westminster Abbey.

particular pattern, which was kept under seal, must have been personally approved by the king. The tomb effigy is of a mature man, with beard and moustache and a distinctively long nose: in the diptych he is shown as a fresh-faced beardless boy, considerably younger than twenty-eight. The plausible solution proposed by several writers[10] is that in the case of the diptych the intention was to show Richard as he looked when he was crowned in his eleventh year.[11]

Technical examination of the king's profile in the painting helps to advance the discussion. With the naked eye, and more clearly with the aid of infra-red reflectography (Fig. 7), it is possible to see that the area of John the Baptist's camel skin which borders on the king's profile was painted at a later stage: it is different in tone and colouring from the rest of the camel skin. Examination under high magnification shows that this area has an underlayer of the green earth used exclusively in the diptych where flesh tones were planned (see p.80). Furthermore, there is an initial black outline to the profile which may be charcoal,

and Richard's profile differs from that of the other figures in having been finally outlined with a thin red orange line rather than a brown one. The inference is that a fairly large patch was allowed for the head, which was blocked in with green earth underpaint but then left, and painted in at a later stage. As the portrait seems not to have been true to the king's appearance at the time, one cannot argue that the artist was waiting to be given a sitting, but rather that he was waiting to be given a pattern. In this instance a pattern showing the king as a young boy was chosen, possibly as he looked when he acceded to the throne and, which is more important, when he was crowned. That Richard was still towards the end of his life very conscious of his extreme youth at his accession is shown by his reference to it in his will drawn up on 16 April 1399.[12]

The deliberate decision to show Richard in the Wilton Diptych as he looked when he was crowned suggests one of the central preoccupations of the diptych. Indeed, the whole interpretation of the diptych hangs on Richard's concept of his kingship.

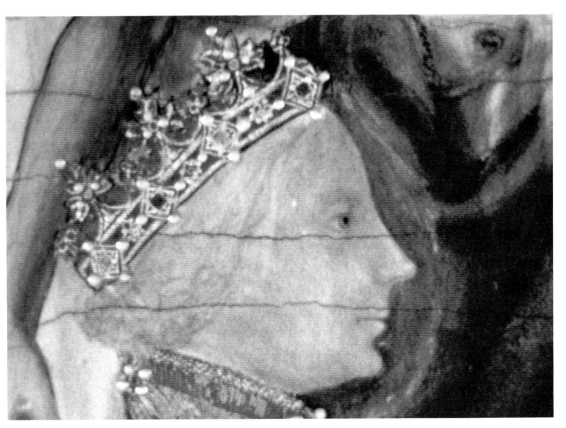

Fig. 7 Infra-red reflectogram of Richard's profile in the Wilton Diptych.

PAGES 25–9

Plate 1 The white hart lying among branches of rosemary on a flowery bank. The exterior of the left wing of the Wilton Diptych.

Plate 2 Richard II with Saints Edmund, Edward the Confessor and John the Baptist. The interior left wing.

Plate 3 The Virgin and Child with Angels. The interior right wing.

Plate 4 The royal arms of England and France ancient impaled with the arms of Edward the Confessor with a helmet, cap of maintenance and lion passant guardant. The exterior of the right wing. For a detail photographed in raking light see Plate 5 on p.29.

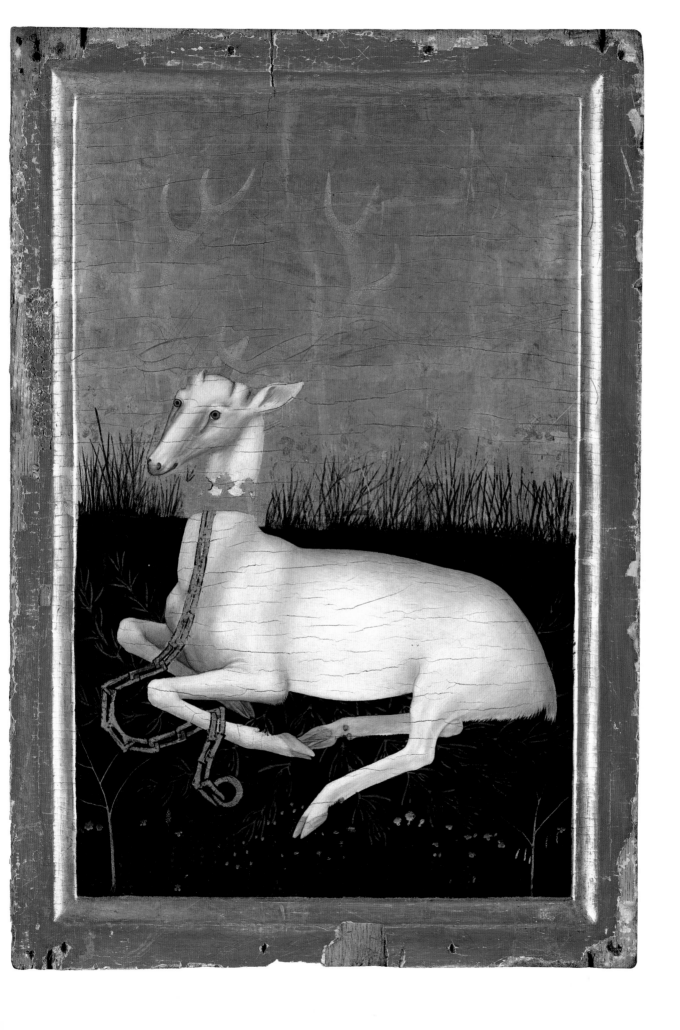

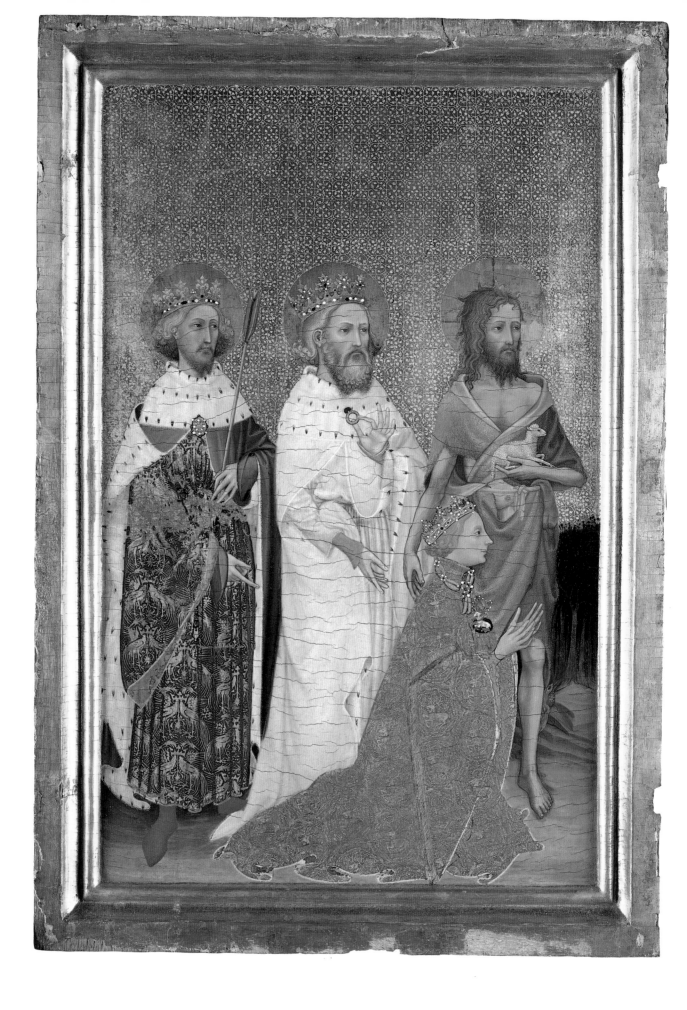

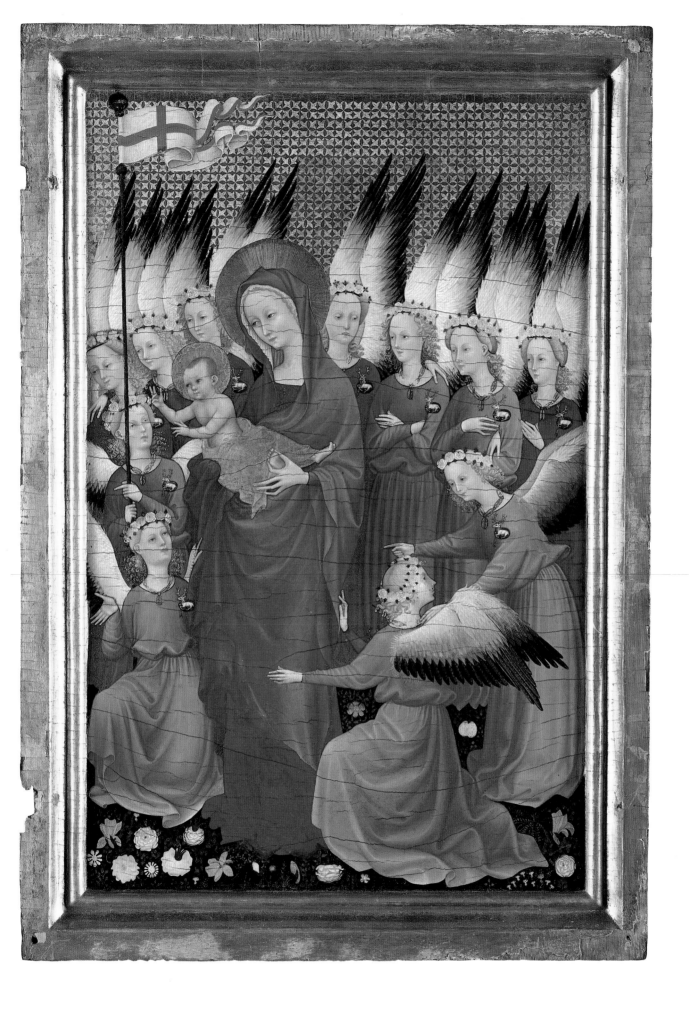

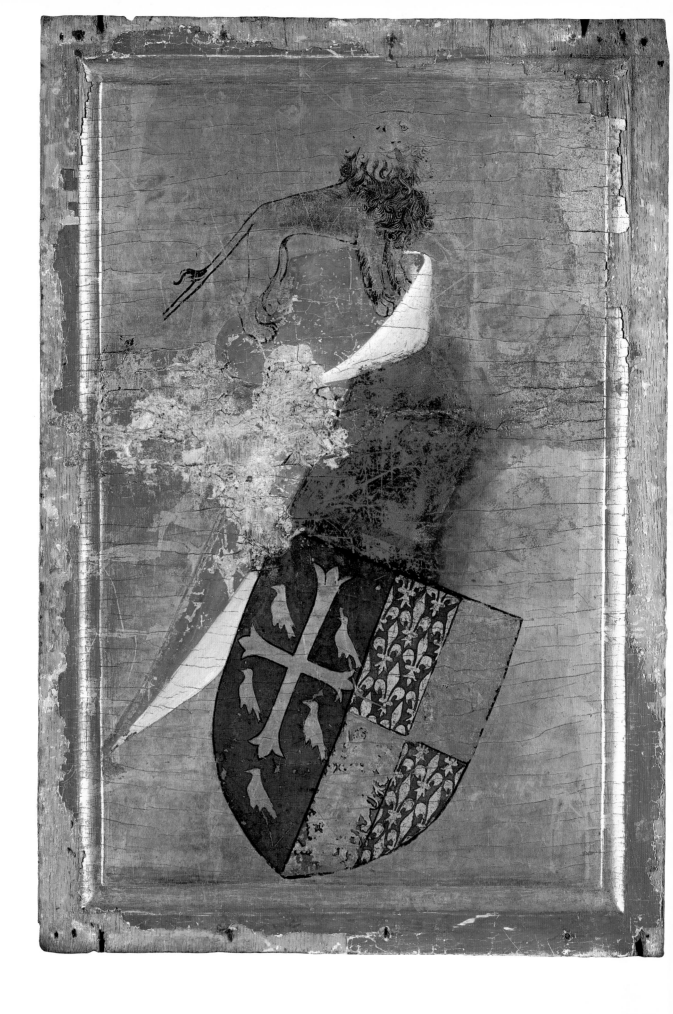

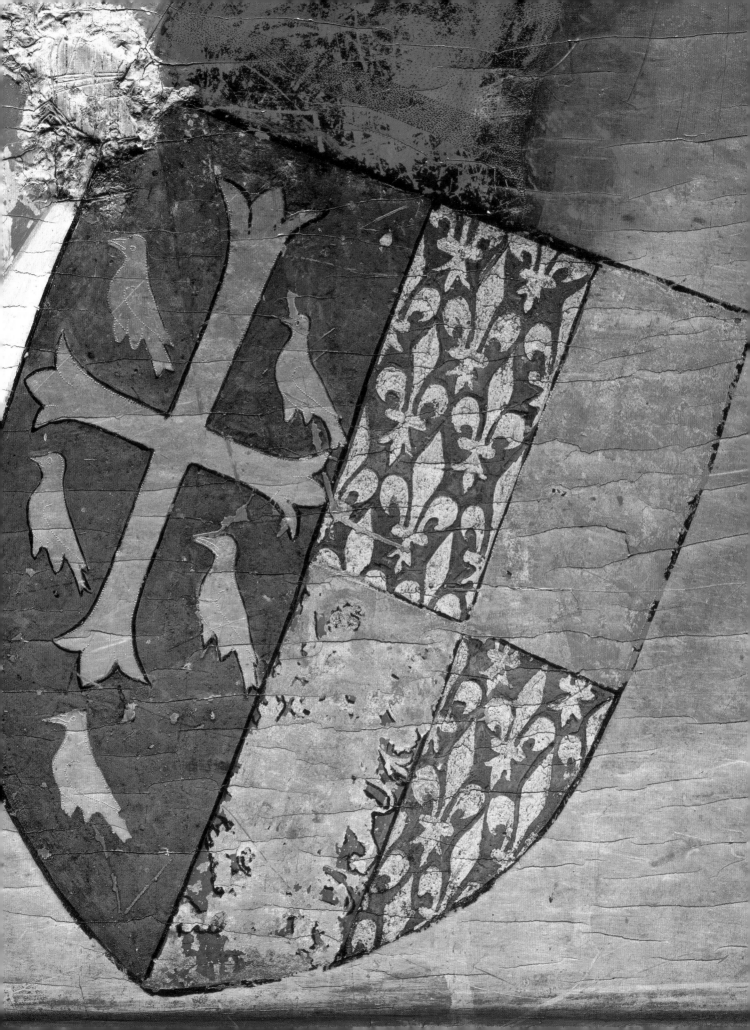

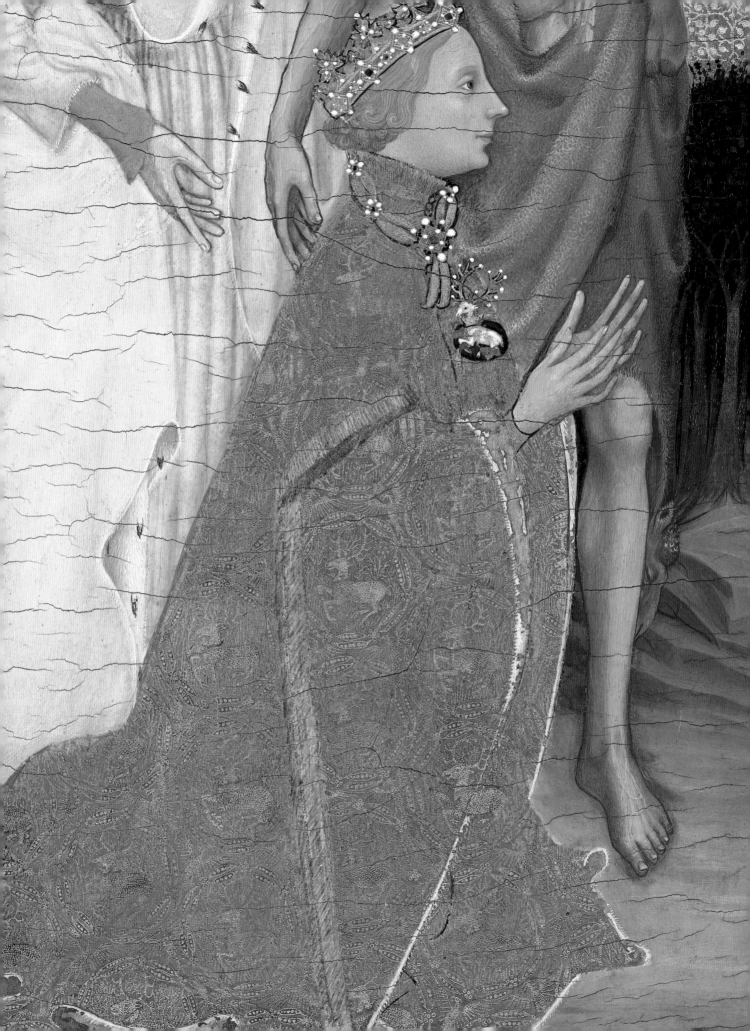

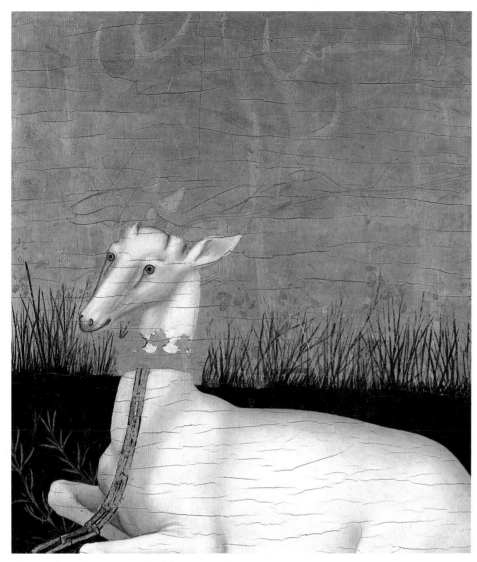

Plate 7 The White Hart. Detail of the exterior of the left wing of the Wilton Diptych.

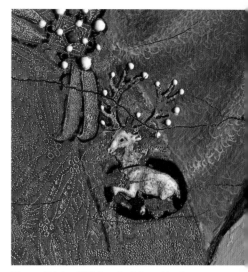

Plate 8 Richard II's jewel of the white hart, with a gold crown around its neck and pearls decorating its antlers. Detail, photographed in raking light.

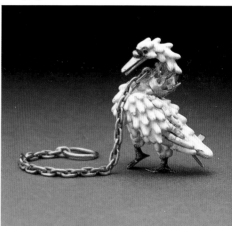

Plate 9 The Dunstable Swan Jewel, *c.*1400. No enamel white harts are known to survive but Richard's jewel must have looked something like this. Gold with white and black enamel, 3.2 × 2.5 cm. London, British Museum.

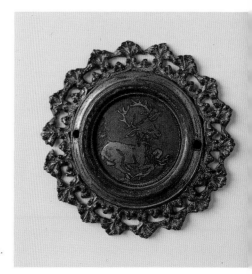

Plate 10 Badge of the white hart, *c.*1377–99, which may have belonged to a follower of Richard II or been a gift from him. Copper alloy, silver and enamel, gilt. Diameter 3.5 cm. Troyes, Musée des Beaux-Arts.

Plate 6 (facing page) King Richard II. Detail of the interior left wing of the Wilton Diptych.

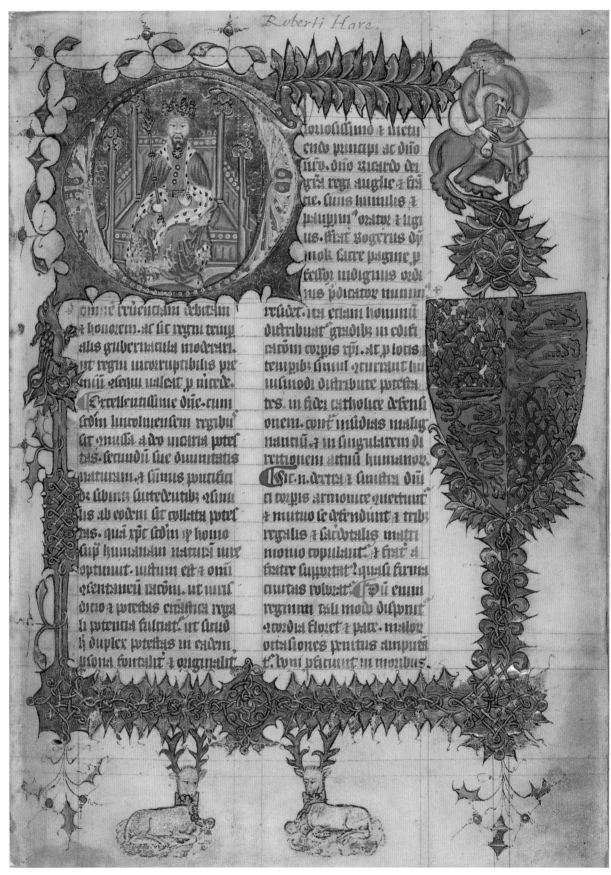

Plate 11 Richard II, the royal arms (here not impaled with those of Edward the Confessor) and two white harts in Dymok's *Liber contra XII Errores et Hereses Lollardorum*, *c.*1395. A presentation copy of the treatise against the heresies of the followers of Wycliffe made for the king. Vellum. Cambridge, Trinity Hall (MS 17, f.1).

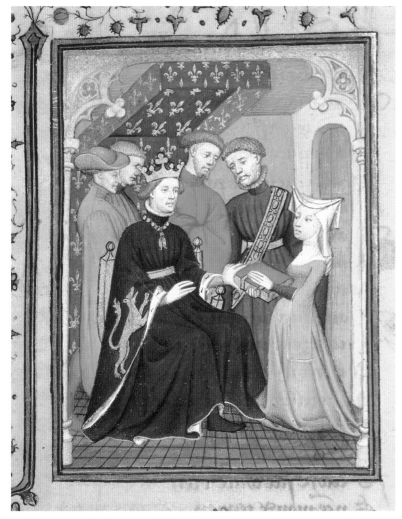

Plate 12 *Charles VI receiving the work of Christine de Pisan*, *c.*1405–10. The French king wears a collar with broomcods. London, British Library (Harley MS 4431, f.178).

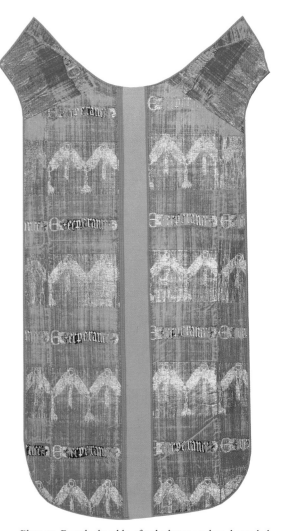

Plate 13 French chasuble of polychrome velvet, brocaded with gold, woven with broomcods and Belts of 'Espérance', thought to have been made during Charles VI's reign, *c.*1400. 118 × 52 cm. Lyons, Musée des Tissus Historiques.

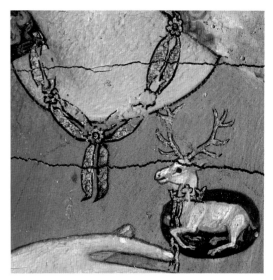

Plate 14 An angel's broomcod collar and white hart badge from the Wilton Diptych. Detail, photographed in raking light.

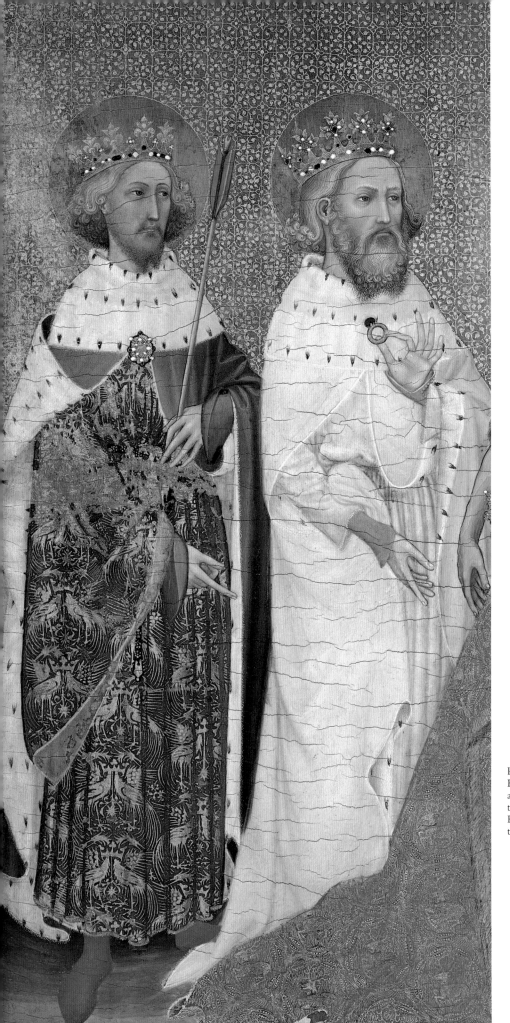

Plate 15 The two royal English saints,
Edmund with the arrow of his martyrdom,
and Edward holding a ring that may refer to
the one he reputedly gave to John the
Evangelist. Detail of the interior left wing of
the Wilton Diptych.

Plate 16 (facing page) *Richard II kneeling before
Saint John the Baptist, c.*1393. John the Baptist
was Richard's patron saint and presents him to
the Virgin and Child in the diptych. Stained
glass, 103 × 65.5 cm. Winchester College.

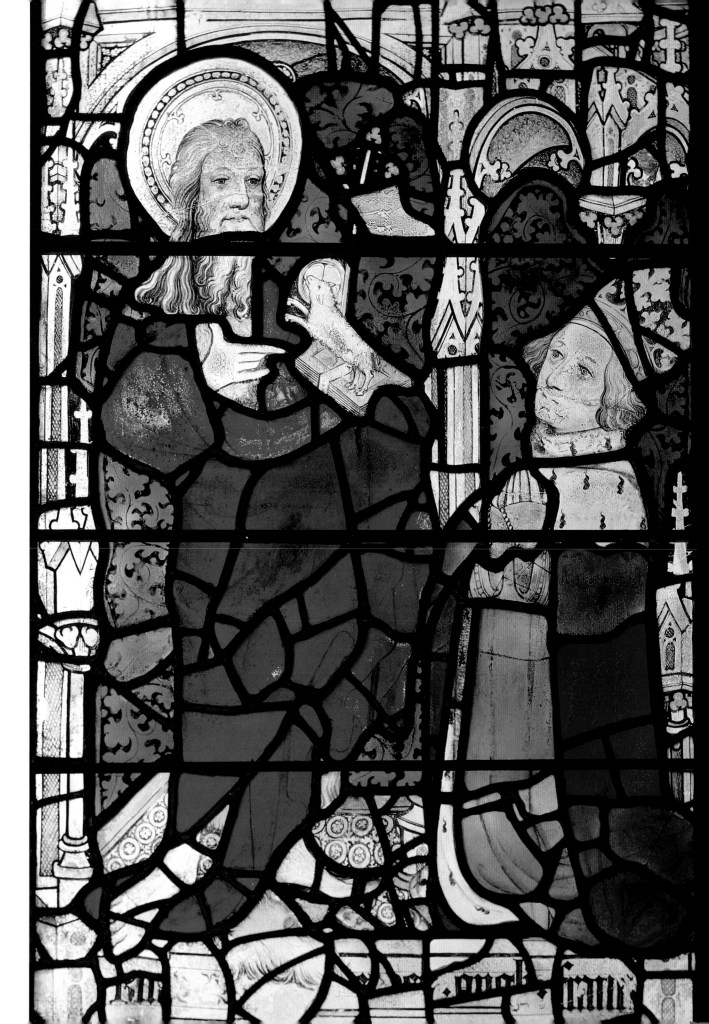

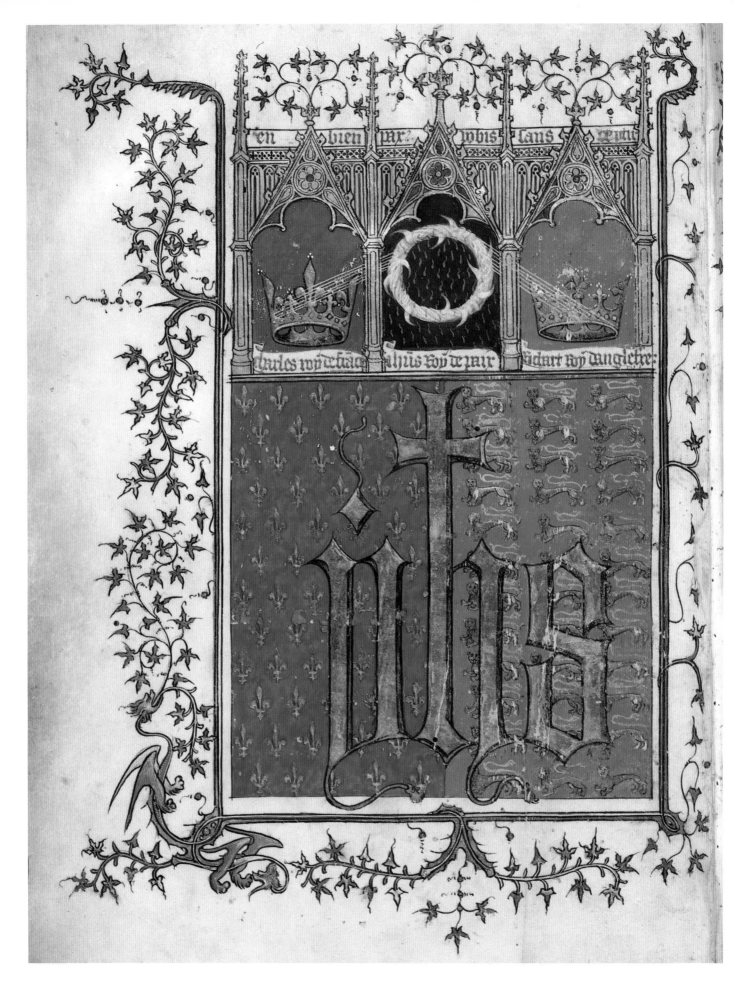

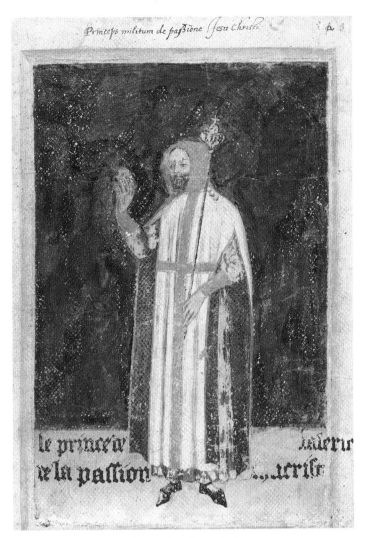

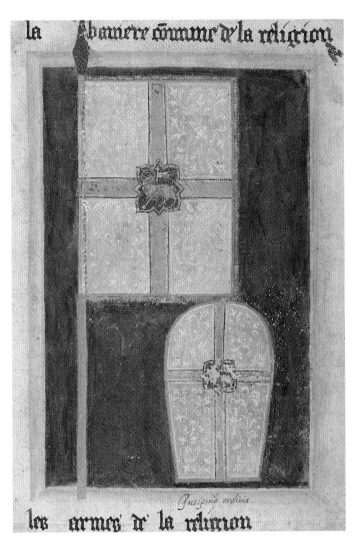

Plate 18 Costume for a prince of the Chevalerie de la Passion de Iehsu Crist, *c*.1395, the chivalric Order proposed in the *Epître de Philippe de Mézières* for a crusade to the Holy Land under the joint leadership of Richard II and Charles VI of France. Oxford, Bodleian Library (MS Ashmole 813, f.2r).

Plate 19 The banner and shield of the Chevalerie de la Passion de Iehsu Crist, which differ markedly from the banner in the diptych. Oxford, Bodleian Library (MS Ashmole 813, f.4r).

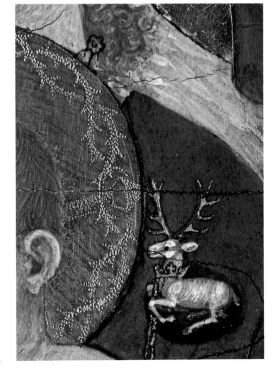

Plate 17 (facing page) The crown of thorns linking the crowns of France (left) and England (right) from the *Epître de Philippe de Mézières*, *c*.1395. This letter to Richard proposed a joint crusade to the Holy Land to be undertaken with Charles VI of France. London, British Library (Royal MS B.VI., f.1v).

Plate 20 Detail of the Christ Child's halo in the Wilton Diptych showing one of the three nails and part of the crown of thorns, symbols of Christ's Passion. Photographed in raking light.

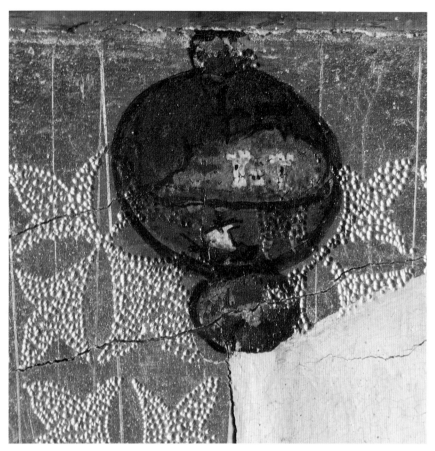

Plate 21 Detail of the orb at the top of the banner in the Wilton Diptych. It contains a green island with trees on the horizon and a white castle with two turrets and black windows. Below is a ship in full sail, on a sea that was originally silver leaf. Photographed in raking light.

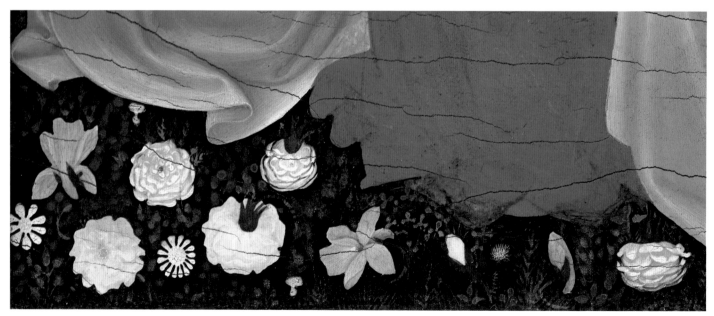

Plate 22 Detail of the flowers in the interior right wing, including strewn roses with their cut stems uppermost, pale blue flowers that may be irises or violets, daisies and mushrooms.

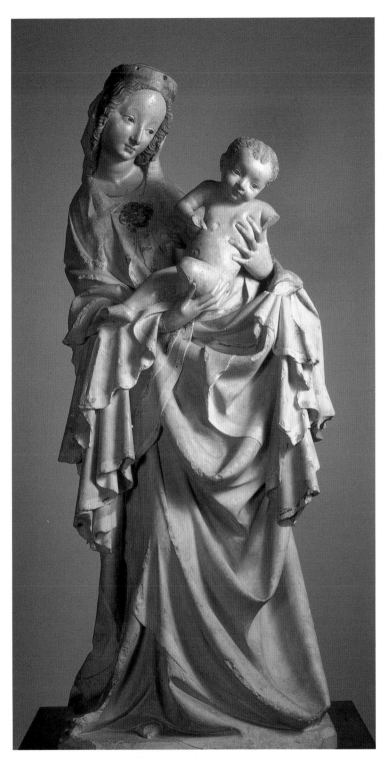

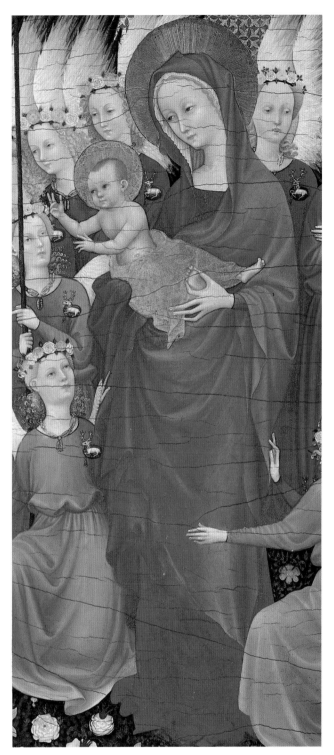

Plate 23 *The Virgin and Child* from Krumlov, in
Bohemia, *c.*1390–1400(?). A similar statue could have
been the model for the Virgin and Child group in
the diptych. Soft limestone, 112 cm high. Vienna,
Kunsthistorisches Museum.

Plate 24 The Virgin and Child and angels. Detail of
the interior right wing of the Wilton Diptych.

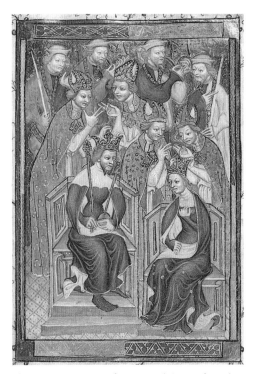

Plate 25 Coronation of a King and Queen from the *Liber Regalis*. *c.*1390–9(?). This book outlining the coronation order was produced during Richard's reign and could even have been made at his request. London, Westminster Abbey (MS 38, p.47).

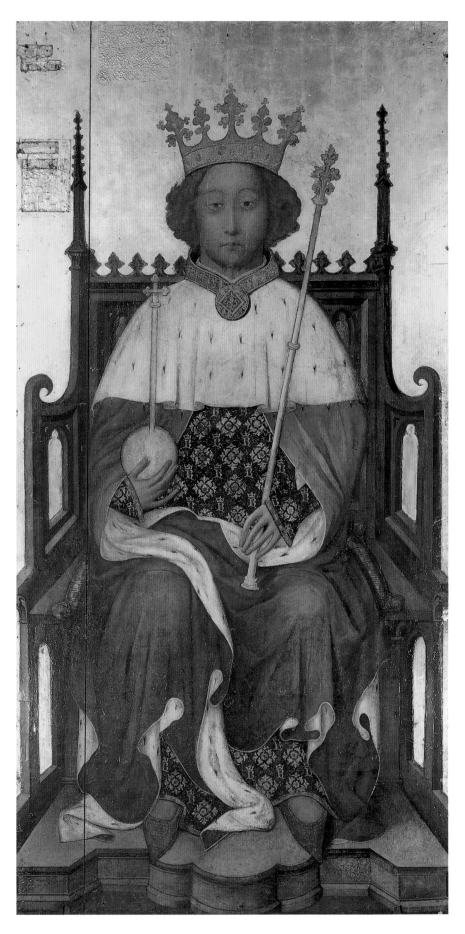

Plate 26 *Richard II Enthroned*, *c.*1395(?). Panel, 213.5 × 110 cm. London, Westminster Abbey.

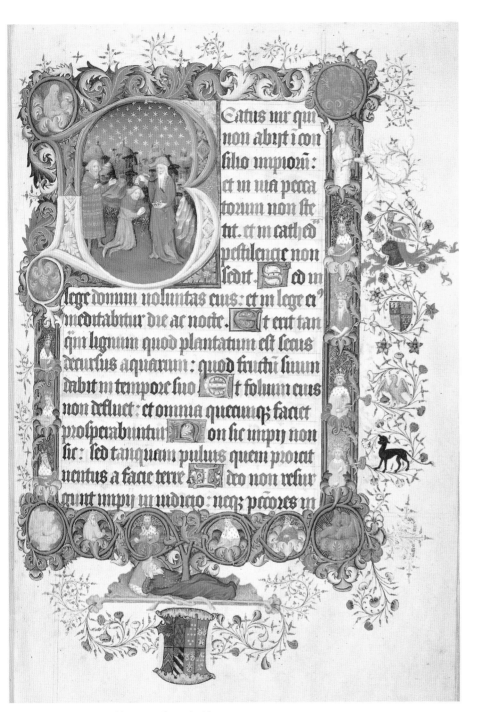

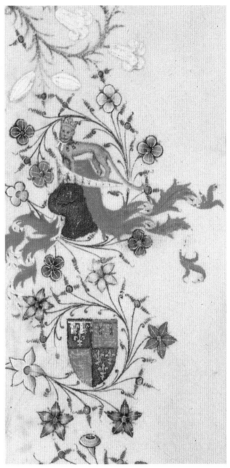

Plate 27 David anointed by Samuel watched by
Jesse, with a border of the Tree of Jesse, from the
Bedford Hours and Psalter, c.1414–23, a manuscript
that has been compared stylistically with the Wilton
Diptych. Illuminated by Herman Scheerre and his
workshop. The Bedford arms are in the margin, the
arms at the bottom are a later addition. London,
British Library (Additional MS 42131, f.73).

Plate 28 Detail of the Bedford arms in the margin
of Plate 27. The arrangement is similar to that of
the arms on the exterior of the Wilton Diptych.

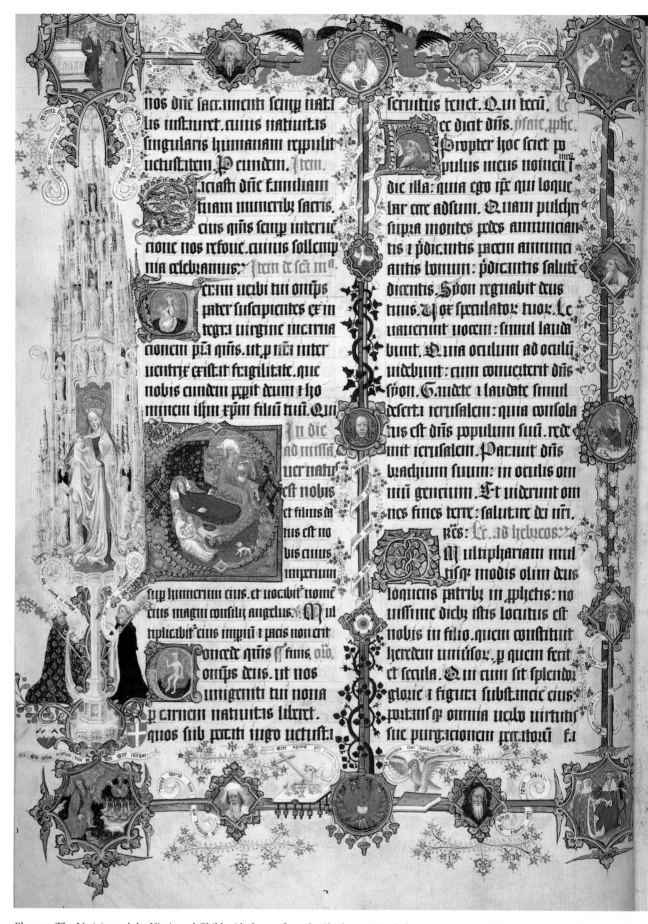

Plate 29 The Nativity and the Virgin and Child with donors from the Sherborne Missal, f.36v. *c.*1395–1407. The manuscript was illuminated by John Siferwas, a Dominican friar, and his workshop, and the scribe was John Whas, a Benedictine monk. The Trustees of the Will of the Ninth Duke of Northumberland (currently on loan to the British Library, Loan MS 82).

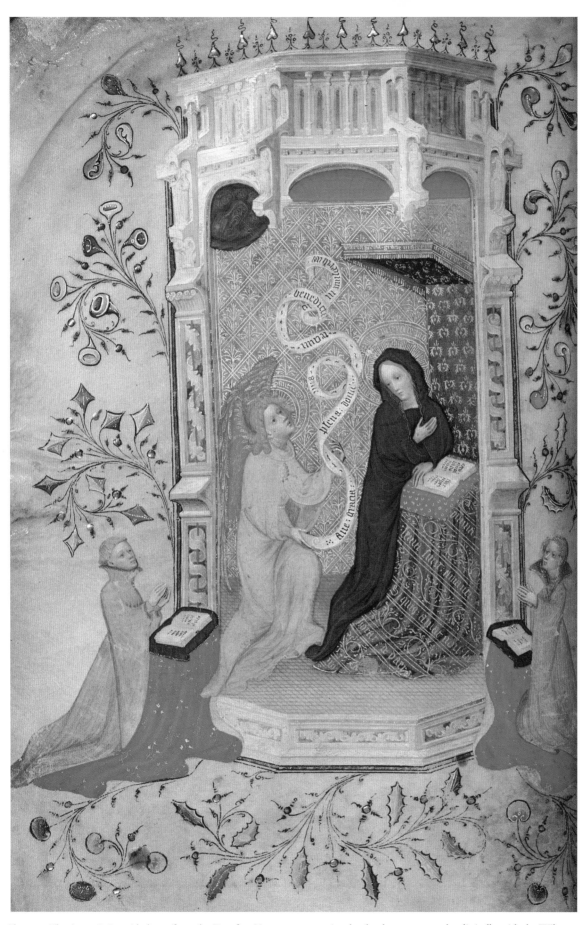

Plate 30 *The Annunciation with donors* from the Beaufort Hours, a manuscript that has been compared stylistically with the Wilton Diptych. Early 15th century. London, British Library (Royal MS 2 A.XVIII, f.23v).

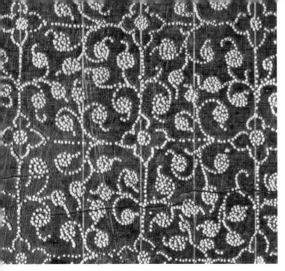

Plate 31 The floral pattern stippled in the gold leaf on the interior left wing. The lines of the grid are plainly visible. Detail, photographed in raking light.

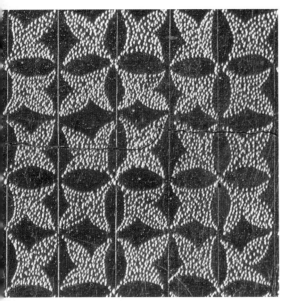

Plate 32 The foliate pattern stippled in the gold leaf on the interior right wing. Detail, photographed in raking light.

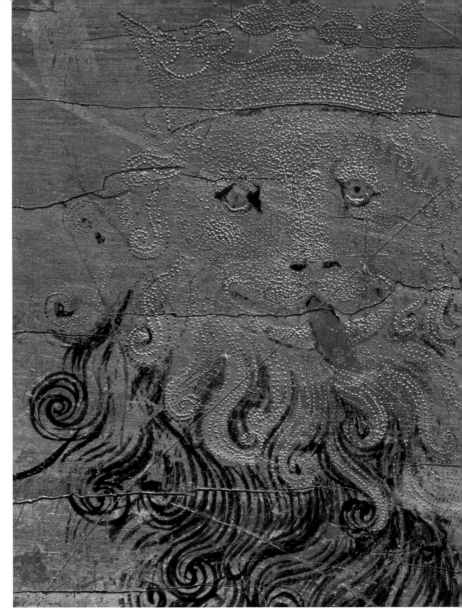

Plate 34 Detail of the lion's face on the exterior of the right wing showing the use of punching for modelling the muzzle and eyes. Photographed in raking light.

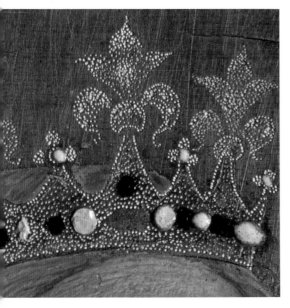

Plate 33 Saint Edmund's crown, stippled so that it stands out from the plain gold surface of his untooled halo. Raised lead white has been used for the pearls, and glazes, which have now darkened, for the jewels. Detail, photographed in raking light.

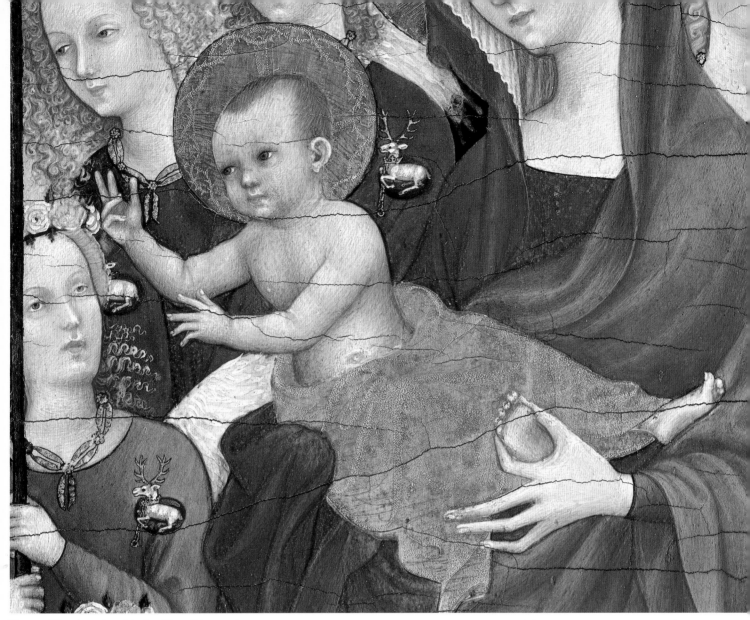

Plate 35 The virtuosity of the handling of the punch
– most evident where it has been used for modelling –
is particularly outstanding in creating the folds of the
Child's robe. Detail, photographed in raking light.

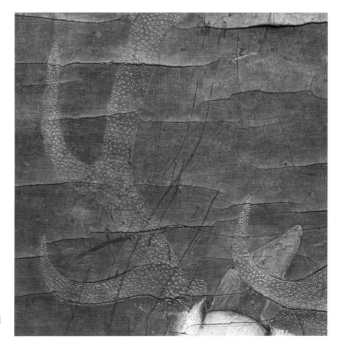

Plate 36 The hart's antlers have been outlined by
incising the gold leaf and then modelled solely by
stippling, relying on the fall of light to make them
stand out from the plain burnished background.
Detail of the exterior of the left wing. Photographed
in raking light.

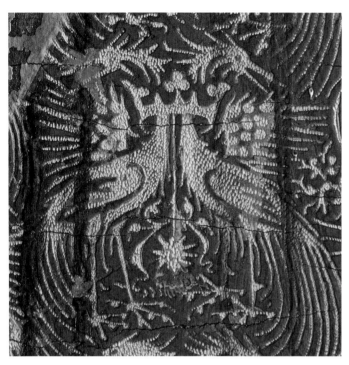

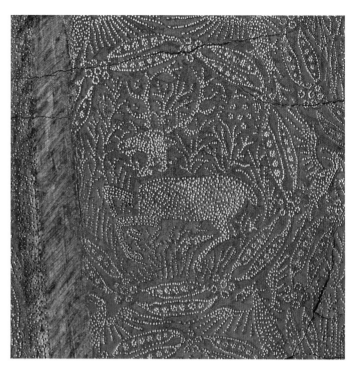

Plate 37 The *sgraffito* design on Saint Edmund's robe of lapis lazuli ultramarine. The blue has been strengthened around the pattern and applied over it to create the vertical folds. Detail, photographed in raking light.

Plate 38 The finely detailed *sgraffito* design on Richard's robe, where vermilion has been scraped away to reveal the gold, which has then been stippled. Detail, photographed in raking light.

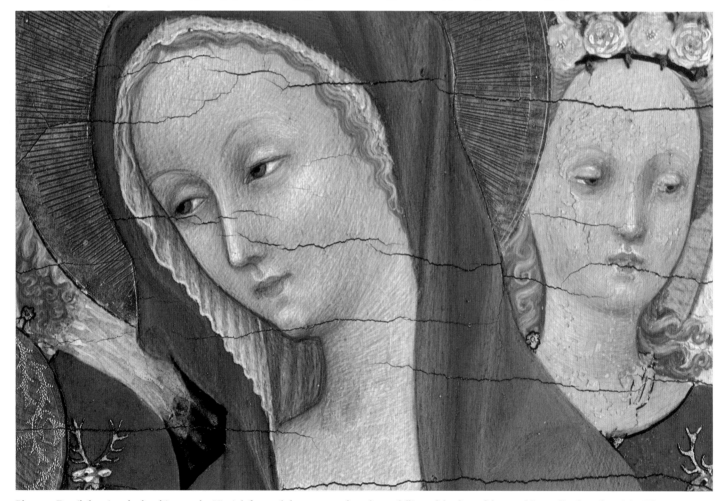

Plate 39 Detail showing the hatching on the Virgin's face and the green earth undermodelling of the face of the angel immediately to her right. The appearance of the painting of the flesh, built up with a series of hatched strokes, is typical of the egg tempera technique. Photographed in raking light.

46

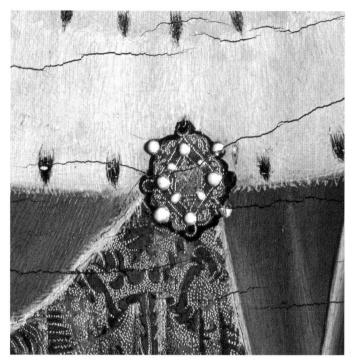

Plate 40 Raised lead white used to achieve the illusion of pearls on Saint Edmund's brooch. Detail, photographed in raking light.

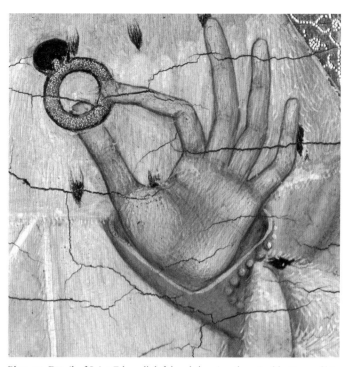

Plate 41 Detail of Saint Edward's left hand showing the raised buttons of his sleeve and the stippling of his ring. Photographed in raking light.

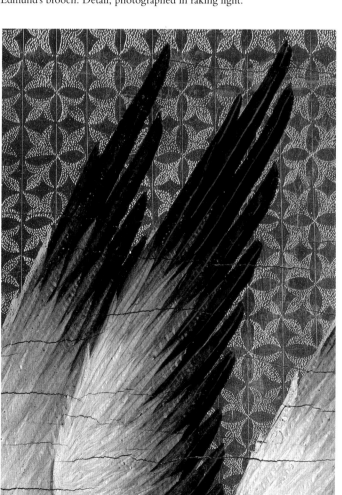

Plate 42 The feathers of the wings of the angel immediately to the right of the Virgin have been picked out with fine red lines. Detail, photographed in raking light.

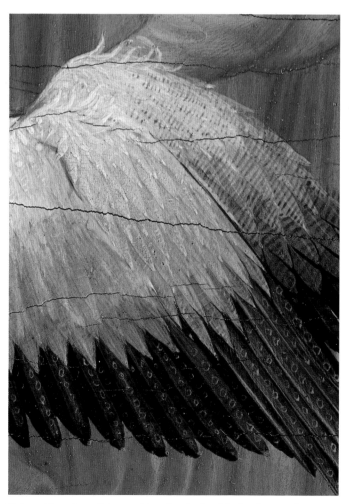

Plate 43 The wings of the angel kneeling in the right-hand corner have a layer of pale pink underpaint and fine green bars on the feathers, not found on the other angels' wings. Detail, photographed in raking light.

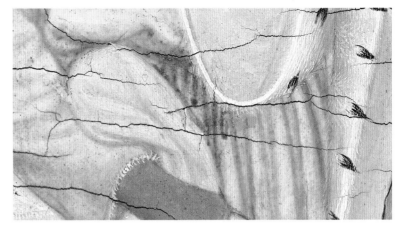

Plate 44 Detail of Saint Edward's robe showing how the red lake pigments have faded, lines of a brownish-red glaze surviving in the shadows and folds.

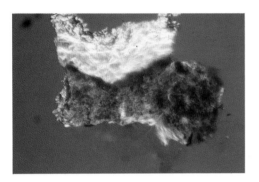

Plate 45 Cross-section of mordant gilding from the blue of the shield on the heraldic panel. The lowest layers are the chalk ground, the orange-red bole for water gilding, and gold leaf. Over these are a thick layer of natural ultramarine blue (bound in glue medium) with a thinner greyish-brown mordant (bound in egg) on top. The final layer of gold leaf attached to the mordant layer is also visible. Magnification 280×.

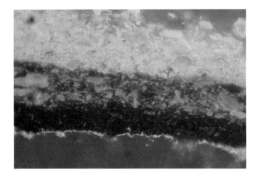

Plate 46 Dark, translucent blue-green paint layer of indigo over gilded background, representing iris leaves on the hart panel. The sample is photographed under the microscope from the top surface, and shows the reflection of light from the gold leaf through the paint. A trace of red-brown bole and chalk ground, beneath the gold, is also visible. Magnification 210×.

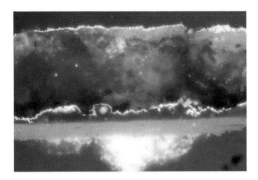

Plate 47 Light grey-green of a small leaf, from the foreground of the Virgin and Child panel, lower edge. The paint here just overlaps the gilding on the integral frame. Over the gold leaf is a dense underlayer of charcoal black, followed by a mid-green composed of indigo and orpiment (mineral arsenic trisulphide). The uppermost paint layer is mainly orpiment with a little indigo. Cross-section, magnification 425×.

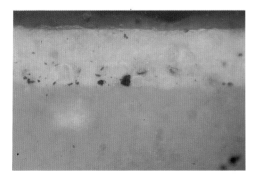

Plate 48 Cross-section from the grey paint of the hart. On the chalk ground there are two layers of paint: a lower light greyish brown composed of white, yellow earth and black, and over this a very pale grey. The paint medium was identified as egg tempera. Magnification 400×.

The White Hart of 'Richart'

As we have seen, the Wilton Diptych is an intensely personal object, closely focused on the king. Richard II is identifiable not only on account of his appearance, but also on account of the prolific use of his personal emblem of the white hart.

At his breast, Richard wears a jewel of a white hart lying on a green background; it has a gold crown around its neck and possibly the faintest trace of a gold chain, with pearls decorating its antlers (Plates 6 and 8). His robe is red, patterned with harts and rosemary encircled by broomcods and interspersed with eagles,[13] all stippled in the gold (Plate 38). White harts which are simpler than the one worn by the king but also on a green background are worn by the angels (Plate 14), indicating a connection between angels and king. Their harts also have chains around their necks. A white hart lying among various plants, including rosemary, with a crown around its neck, and with a chain hanging from the crown, is painted on the exterior of the diptych (Plates 1 and 7).

The white hart is thought to have been inherited from Richard's mother, Joan of Kent.[14] Richard may have adopted it as his personal emblem because of the implicit pun on his own name – most evident in its spelling in French 'Richart'. He seems to have begun using it as an emblem in the form of jewellery early in his reign: in 1379 he pledged various jewels with the City of London as security for a loan, including two brooches with white harts in the middle and three brooches in the shape of white harts; in 1382 he asked to borrow them back for his marriage to Anne of Bohemia.[15] He first publicly adopted the white hart with a crown and golden chain at a tournament in Smithfield in 1390.[16] The fact that brooches of the white hart were in frequent use at the court is shown by accounts of the King's Wardrobe dating from 1393–4, which include a payment to a goldsmith for the mending and re-enamelling of two harts of gold.[17]

The white hart badge worn at Richard's breast in the Wilton Diptych shows up densely on X-radiographs (see Fig. 26). It has been thickly painted in raised layers of lead white to achieve a sculptural quality, creating the impression of a jewel, and is almost certainly intended to appear as if made of *émail en ronde bosse* (opaque white enamel fused over gold). This difficult and expensive technique seems to have been perfected in Paris towards the second half of the fourteenth century,[18] although it was also practised by goldsmiths in England. As far as we know, no such enamel white harts survive, but Richard's original

jewel must have looked something like the Dunstable Swan Jewel (Plate 9).[19] A jewelled hart similar to Richard's, particularly with regard to the green background and the pearls decorating the antlers, occurs in the inventory of the royal treasure made in the first year of the reign of Henry IV.[20]

It was customary in the Middle Ages for the emblems or badges of kings and nobles to be worn by their followers and supporters, including servants, as a visible declaration of allegiance.[21] For example, in 1397 the sheriff of Kent was ordered to proclaim that all 'lords, esquires and gentlemen who wear the king's livery of the hart' were to ride with the king to Westminster Palace and remain to serve as long as required.[22] Badges of livery were also given as signs of favour: in 1392 Richard wrote to the Doge of Venice saying that he had bestowed on a knight the privilege of wearing the badge of the hart as was the custom for knights serving at his side.[23] So powerful was the sense of allegiance generated by the wearing of emblems, and so dangerous the potential for divisive loyalties, that the first Parliament of Henry IV legislated to forbid any subject of whatever rank to use or give any livery or badge of company; the king alone would have the right to grant his livery to whom he chose and it was to be worn only in his presence unless abroad or in times of war.[24]

Presumably the type of hart worn by supporters depended on their rank and wealth. The angels in the right wing of the diptych wear white harts, indicating that they are supporters of the king, but their harts are more flatly painted than that of Richard, and lack pearls on the antlers. None the less, the harts are still intended to appear three-dimensional, as is evident from the antlers peeping over the shoulder of the kneeling angel on the right, and therefore still intended to represent jewels.

A number of jewels of the white hart have been recorded in the possession of members of the English and French courts; the ones in France were presumably gifts from Richard. In 1392 a white enamel hart was given to the Countess of Derby by her husband.[25] In his will of 1397 John of Gaunt bequeathed to his wife his best hart with his best collar, and his second best hart to his daughter, Philippa, Queen of Portugal.[26] Other jewels of the white hart are recorded abroad: in 1405 Margaret of Flanders, wife of Philip, Duke of Burgundy, owned a white hart lodged 'de la devise du Roy d'Angleterre' (of the device of the King of England), decorated with pearls, a sapphire, rubies and diamonds.[27] Although no jewels of the white hart are known, an enamel badge of a white hart (Plate 10) has survived which might have

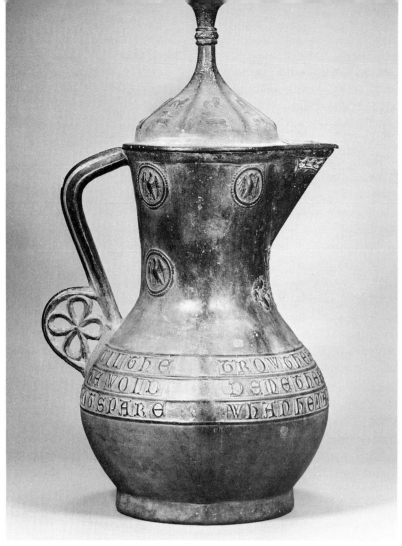

Fig. 8 Jug with royal arms and badges, with harts on the lid and a crown on the spout, 1377–99. Copper alloy, 40.2 cm high. London, British Museum.

Fig. 9 *The White Hart*, c.1377–99. Wall painting in the Muniment Room of Westminster Abbey.

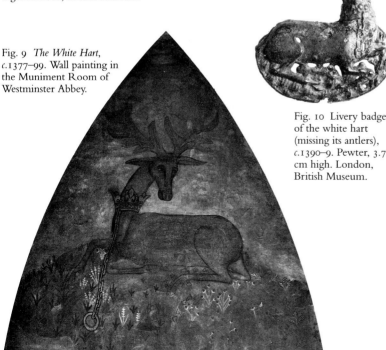

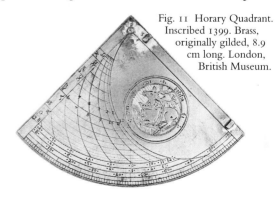

Fig. 10 Livery badge of the white hart (missing its antlers), c.1390–9. Pewter, 3.7 cm high. London, British Museum.

belonged to a follower of King Richard or been a gift from him.[28]

The survival of a number of pewter badges of the white hart (Fig. 10)[29] and of a mould for making base metal hart badges (in the Norfolk County Museum[30]) suggests that badges worn by the rank and file who supported the king with visible allegiance were of cheaper materials. In *Mum and the Sothsegger,* a satirical poem written around 1399, it is said that Richard's retainers were 'laverers . . . that had hertis on hie on her brestis . . . they bare hem the bolder for her gay broches' (workers who wore harts high on their breasts and they bore themselves boldly because of their gay brooches), and the pun is made that for every badge of the white hart bestowed the king lost scores of faithful hearts.[31]

As well as being worn as jewels or badges, emblems decorated all sorts of items used at court, such as plate,[32] articles of daily use (Figs. 8 and 11),[33] manuscripts (see Plate 11),[34] banners, the royal barge,[35] textiles,[36] seals.[37] White harts decorated buildings associated with Richard, either carved in the stonework, as at Westminster Hall,[38] Westminster Abbey,[39] and York Minster;[40] or painted on walls, as in the great chapel in the Old Manor at Windsor Park,[41] and in Westminster Abbey (Fig. 9),[42] or on columns, as on those flanking the tomb of Edward II (died 1327), whom Richard was trying to have canonised;[43] or in stained-glass windows.[44] The white hart also occurs on the corbel of the canopy over the two recumbent figures in the memorial brass of Sir Simon Felbrigg (died 1443), standard bearer to Richard from 1395 (Fig. 15).[45]

The painter of the diptych would almost certainly have had a live animal to study. In 1393 a white hart was given to the king by Sir Stephen Scrope and kept at Windsor.[46] Not only is the large hart on the exterior of the diptych realistically depicted as if studied from life, but also the anatomy of all the harts is carefully studied on a minute scale.

There is therefore abundant evidence for Richard's use of the white hart as his personal emblem. However, what is puzzling in the diptych is the almost equal prominence given to the motif of the broom plant.

Fig. 11 Horary Quadrant. Inscribed 1399. Brass, originally gilded, 8.9 cm long. London, British Museum.

The planta genista *– a Plantagenet Emblem?*

Much in the same way that Richard used the white hart, Charles VI of France used the broomcod as one of his emblems. Its presence helps to date the diptych, since it seems highly unlikely that it would have been adopted before relations between England and France became friendlier, around 1395–6. Ultimately it was taken over by Richard II and was adopted as an emblem by later English kings. But was the broomcod used in the Wilton Diptych to signal alliance with the French king, or is it there as Richard's personal emblem? And why has it been given almost equal prominence with the white hart?

Broomcods encircle the harts on Richard's robe (Plate 38) and around his neck Richard wears a gold collar of broomcods, consisting of a double row of pods connected by white flowers with green centres, and a square clasp with a blue jewel at the centre and green stones and pearls around the outside (see Plate 6). The angels wear similar but simpler gold collars (see Plate 14).

Livery collars probably began as a French fashion, becoming popular among the English aristocracy towards the end of the fourteenth century. Exchanges of collars could symbolise friendship: for example, in 1394 the Earl of Arundel complained that Richard II unduly favoured his uncle, John of Gaunt, even to the extent of wearing Gaunt's livery collar.[47]

The evidence that the broomcod was the livery of the French king, Charles VI, is extensive.[48] Its origins are obscure, but the collar of the *cosse de genêt* (pod of broom) was in use at the French court by 1378, when Charles V is said to have granted it to his chamberlain.[49] However, it was Charles VI who took up the emblem of the broom plant and made it his own.[50] Numerous examples of its use are recorded at the French court,[51] and a chasuble now in Lyons (Plate 13), embroidered with broomcods alternating with the motif of the Bourbon Order of the Belt of Hope ('Espérance'), is thought to have been made during Charles's reign.[52]

There are also visual records of broomcod collars being worn at the French court.[53] For example, Charles VI is shown wearing one in a manuscript dating from around 1410 (Plate 12).[54] A number of such collars are described in the inventories of the French royal family as being made of white and green enamel, and ornamented with pearls, rubies and diamonds.[55] An average of twenty persons a year received a collar of broomcods from Charles VI as a sign of royal favour in the years for which records survive (1388, 1390, 1399, 1400).[56]

It is almost certain that Richard II imitated the use of the *cosse de genêt* from the French court, and that this usage is extremely unlikely to date from earlier than 1395 when negotiations were underway for the widowed Richard to take as his second wife the six-year-old daughter of Charles VI (born 9 November 1389). It was probably at this amicable point in relations between the two courts that various broomcod collars first came into Richard's possession. In 1396, when Richard married his child bride, Charles VI gave Richard a gold collar of broomcods identical to one he had made for himself by a Parisian goldsmith.

The description of the collar made for the French king still survives in a transcription of the accounts of the king's goldsmith,[57] but it is clear that it is not the same as the one worn by Richard in the Wilton Diptych. The key differences are the lack of pendant letters and of two pounced gold rolls, the lack of pearls set like peas within the pods, and in particular the lack of any enamelling on the pods.[58] Nor does Richard's collar resemble either of the two broomcod collars brought from France by Isabelle when she came to England in 1396.[59]

Whatever the significance of the broomcods in the Wilton Diptych, their extensive presence suggests that it is unlikely to have been painted before the beginning of the marriage negotiations in February 1395.[60] The marriage took place by proxy in Paris in March 1396. When the two kings met at Ardres in October 1396 to conclude the negotiations, the weeping child, whose dolls were included in her wedding trousseau, was handed over to her English husband. Both kings were similarly attired in a red velvet gown, with a collar of the livery of the French king, and a great hart on the arm, and it has been pointed out that this is how Richard appears in the diptych.[61]

We know of another instance of a similar combination of the white hart and broomcods connected with the royal marriage: in January 1397 Richard paid for robes for twenty ladies to lead twenty armed men from the Tower of London to Smithfield after the coronation of Isabelle. The robes, designed by the court painter, Thomas Lytlington, were long gowns of red tartaryn silk with white harts of silver with crowns and chains of gold lying among broom plants; there were twenty short gowns of the same design for the armed men – and it has been noted that the pattern on Richard's robe in the Wilton Diptych bears a very similar design.[62] In both these instances the visual coincidences with the diptych are very strong and further support the suggestion that it probably dates from sometime after 1396/7.

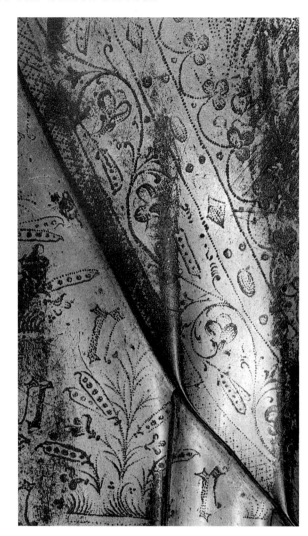

Fig. 12 Detail of the pouncing showing broomcods on Richard II's robes in his tomb effigy in Westminster Abbey.

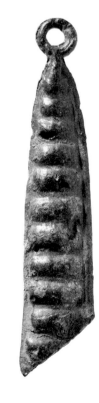

Fig. 13 Broompod livery badge, late 14th/early 15th century. Pewter, 6.4 cm high. Salisbury and South Wiltshire Museum.

It was customary for a husband to take over his wife's emblems.[63] Richard seems to have taken over rosemary, emblem of his first wife, Anne of Bohemia, and when on his marriage to Isabelle he exchanged gifts with Charles VI, Richard gave him a collar of the livery of the dead queen, presumably rosemary.[64] This would seem a strange gesture, unless one can argue that Richard considered it *his* livery by virtue of his marriage. Certainly its combination with the white hart on the exterior of the diptych, in the context of heraldic emblems personal to him, suggests that he used it as his own. Similarly, he could have considered the broomcod collar his livery by virtue of his marriage to Isabelle.

It is also possible to argue that Richard adopted the broom plant as an emblem for much the same reason as he made the white hart his own. The Latin for broom plant is *planta genista,* and it has been suggested that the kings of England took up this emblem in reference to the name Plantagenet – the family name of English monarchs from 1154 to 1485.[65] If Richard indeed adopted the white hart as an emblem in reference to his own name, then he would very probably have been alert to the allusion of the *planta genista.* Certainly Richard had broomcods and broom plants pounced alongside his other personal emblems of the white hart and the sunburst on his robes on his tomb effigy (Fig. 12) – the tomb in which he planned to be buried, not with Isabelle of France but with his first wife, Anne of Bohemia. The broomcods on the effigy are very like those on the diptych, with the seeds rendered as little rosettes decorating the neckline much like a broomcod collar. The tomb effigies were commissioned in April 1395,[66] and the pouncing of the robes was probably among the last things to be done – almost certainly in mid-1399.

Further evidence that the broom plant was rapidly absorbed into the complement of royal badges is provided by the memorial brass on the tomb of Sir John Golafre in Westminster Abbey, who died in 1396. This shows a white hart lodged among broom plants in the surviving pattern of the border.[67] Sir John Golafre was close to the king, being one of his Chamber Knights from 1385 to 1395,[68] and his possessions were among those inventoried with the king's in 1400.[69] Similarly, the broom plant is included, together with the emblem of a swan, in the sepulchral brass in Westminster Abbey of Eleanor de Bohun (died 1399), daughter of Humphrey de Bohun, Constable of England, and wife of Thomas of Woodstock, Duke of Gloucester, one of Richard's uncles.[70]

The evidence therefore suggests that Richard, having acquired collars from the French royal house, and having assimilated the broom plant as an emblem, began to wear the broomcod collar as his own. The inventories of Richard's jewellery, drawn up after his deposition, itemise three broomcod collars,[71] and describe them as the livery of the kings of France; none of them resembles those recorded as having been given by Charles or brought by Isabelle. The heaviest of the three is described as 'one collar of the livery of the king of France with one good square balas ruby between good round pearls and six other good pearls between two pods of broom'.[72] This collar seems to be similar to that worn by Richard II in the Wilton Diptych, but the description is too vague to be certain. However, the fact that Richard's collar in the diptych and those in the inventories were so very different from those described as coming from France suggests that Richard commissioned his own collars,[73] deliberately different, and that the one shown in the diptych is the result of such a commission.

Evidence that broomcod collars were being made in England is to be found in the inventory of Isabelle's possessions which the French claimed back in 1400: there it is stated that Isabelle had a collar which had been given to her by the Duke of Albemarle (that is, Edward of York, who was Duke of Albemarle from September 1397), consisting of broomcods with roundels of rosemary and an ostrich – both emblems of Anne of Bohemia.[74] This combination of broomcods with two emblems of the dead queen strongly suggests that the collar was of English manufacture and that it was in use at the English court.

Use of the broom plant by subsequent kings confirms the view that in his last few years Richard had established the broom plant as an English royal emblem. Henry IV (r. 1399–1413) used it, presumably as part of his attempt to legitimise his accession: in the procession from the Tower of London to Westminster on the eve of his coronation he was, according to the French chronicler Froissart, wearing a collar of the livery of the king of France, that is a broomcod collar.[75] In 1401 he included broom plants in the stained-glass windows of Eltham palace.[76] In 1426 Henry VI had a collar made of links of Lancastrian Ss joined with broomcods.[77]

Furthermore, a few surviving broomcods made of pewter (Fig. 13) have been found in England. These are extremely unlikely to be French. Although their date is uncertain, it is quite possible that they were made in the reign of Richard II.[78] They suggest that the broomcod made of base metal, like the pewter badge of the white hart, was worn as a token of allegiance by the lower ranks of Richard's supporters

In conclusion it may be said that although initially a French emblem, the broom plant was quickly adopted into the corpus of English royal emblems, and that its use, having a special significance for the Plantagenets, persisted. If this is so, the broomcod motif was included in the Wilton Diptych not only as a sign of friendship and alliance with Charles, but also as a symbol of Richard's Plantagenet descent. It would thus be yet another instance of Richard's preoccupation with his own kingship which is so central to the meaning of the diptych.

The Three Saints and the Adoration of the King

The combination of saints shown with Richard in the left wing is unique to the diptych. The two English royal saints, Edmund and Edward, and Saint John the Baptist, were chosen because of their particular significance for Richard's kingship, and their combined presence has an added meaning which may indicate the original purpose of the diptych.

SAINT EDMUND This English royal saint (Plate 15) stands at the extreme left, wearing a green ermine-lined cloak over a gold and blue robe patterned with birds, and under that a blue-sleeved robe. In his left hand he holds an arrow – the tip of which, probably originally of silverleaf, has now largely disappeared.

Edmund was the last king of East Anglia (841–69/70), martyred when defeated by the Danes for refusing to deny the Christian faith. He is traditionally said to have been killed with arrows. He was buried in Norfolk and around 915 his body was transferred to the Benedictine monastery later called Bury St Edmunds. In 1095 his body was moved again to a new church and in 1198 re-enshrined. The shrine became a focus for pilgrims and a cult grew up around it: there are a number of pilgrim badges showing either the saint (Fig. 14), or a sheaf of arrows in reference to his martyrdom.[79] Edmund was widely venerated together with Saint Edward and Saint George as one of the patron saints of England.[80]

Richard's devotion to him is reasonably well documented. Edmund may have had particular significance for Richard's kingship, since Richard would very likely have identified strongly with him as another ruler who became king at a young age, in Edmund's case supposedly at the age of fifteen. Richard visited Bury St Edmunds in 1383, and the inventory of Westminster Abbey of 1388 shows that he gave the abbey a gift of three banners, including one of Saint Edmund.[81] The saint's slippers formed part of the coronation regalia which Richard wore when he was crowned. One slipper fell off immediately after the

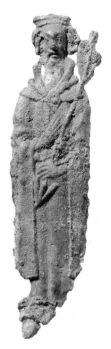

Fig. 14 Saint Edmund holding an arrow. Pilgrim badge, early 15th century. Pewter, 5.7 cm high. Salisbury and South Wiltshire Museum.

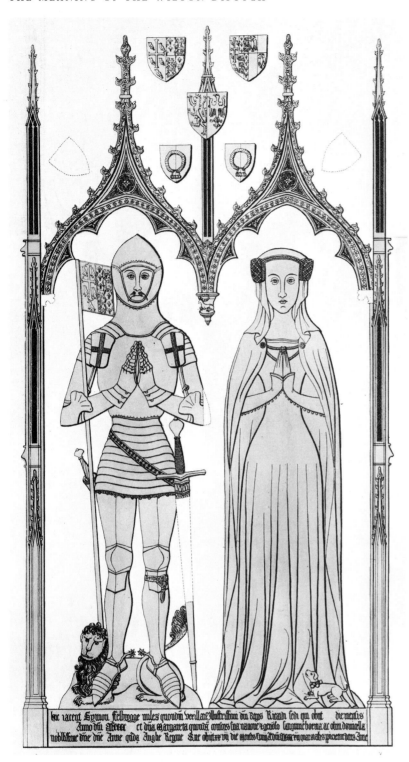

Fig. 15 The sepulchral brass of Richard's standard bearer, Sir Simon Felbrigg (d.1443), and his wife (d.1416), in Felbrigg Church, Norfolk. 19th-century engraving. Society of Antiquaries of London.

ceremony and in 1390 Richard presented to the regalia a pair embroidered in pearls, with fleurs-de-lis, which had been blessed by Pope Urban VI.[82] Edmund is, therefore, like much else in the diptych, linked to Westminster Abbey, and in particular to the coronation service.

Edmund's robe (see Plate 37) is a reminder that every detail in the diptych is germane to the main theme: the birds in the pattern of the robe are linked back to back not by the usual simple rings commonly found in such fabrics, but by crowns.

SAINT EDWARD THE CONFESSOR Next to Saint Edmund stands Edward the Confessor, to whom Richard was fervently devoted. Edward is wearing an ermine-lined cloak which was originally pink over a darker red robe (see p.80), and blue sleeves, and holding a ring with a blue stone (Plate 41). The ring refers to the legend that Edward the Confessor gave a ring to a poor pilgrim who turned out to be Saint John the Evangelist. It may also represent the ring, said to have belonged to Edward the Confessor, which was described in an inventory of Westminster Abbey taken in 1388 as adorned with one sapphire and eight red stones in the custody of the abbot.[83]

Edward, the son of Ethelred the Unready, was the last of the Anglo-Saxon line. He was king of England from 1042 to 1066, and died on 5 January, the eve of Richard II's birthday. His reputation for holiness began during his lifetime, and he was canonised in 1161. He was the virtual founder of Westminster Abbey where he was buried. His relics were moved by Henry III in 1269 to a new tomb in the Abbey which became a national shrine and focus of pilgrimage.[84] A range of badges is associated with his cult. He was considered the patron saint of England, together with Saint Edmund, until gradually superseded by Saint George.

Edward's cult, which had been fostered by Henry III,[85] was taken up with great fervour by Richard. Around 1395 he had the royal arms impaled with those of Edward; it seems that after the death of his first wife, Anne of Bohemia, Richard turned his devotion to the saint. The impaled arms are shown on the exterior of the diptych (Plates 4 and 5), as well as on numerous objects associated with Richard and his court,[86] such as the standard held by Richard's standard-bearer, Sir Simon Felbrigg (Fig. 15), and, more significantly, the canopy above Richard's head in his tomb effigy in Westminster Abbey (Fig. 16). Richard went to pray at Saint Edward's shrine in the Abbey in times of crisis, for example before riding out in June 1381 to confront the rebels led by Wat Tyler at Smithfield, and in 1397 members of Parliament had to swear

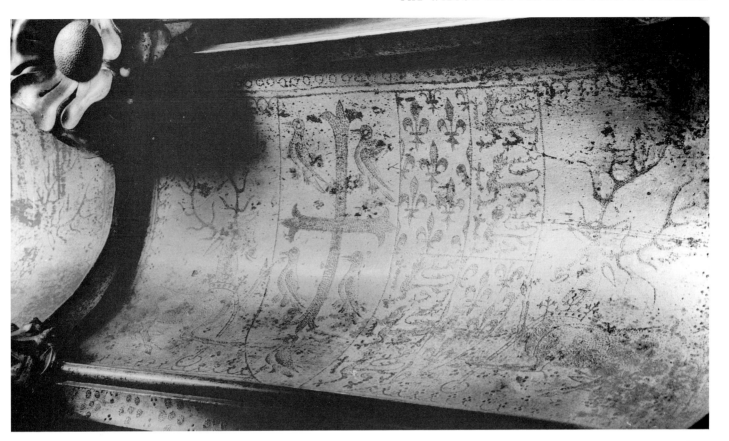

Fig. 16 Detail of the pouncing on the canopy above Richard's head in the tomb at Westminster Abbey showing the royal arms impaled with those of Edward the Confessor and white harts.

their support for Richard at the shrine. He also worshipped there on the feast of the Translation of Saint Edward (13 October) in 1390, attending Prime, Vespers and Compline, Matins at midnight and a procession during the day, and at High Mass he sat in the choir wearing his crown.[87]

Edward the Confessor was central to the ceremony of the coronation. Richard was said to have been crowned clad with the coat of the saint,[88] and his crown was used for the coronation ceremony.[89] Moreover, part of the ceremony detailed in the *Liber Regalis*, a book probably produced in Richard's reign (see p.61 and Plate 25) giving a version of the coronation order, involved the king and queen going to the shrine of Saint Edward at the end of Mass and laying their crowns on the altar. At this point the king divested himself of his coronation robes and shoes, as well as of the regalia, which were returned to the custody of the abbot, with the exception of the sceptre; the king and queen then received different crowns and robes for leaving the Abbey.[90]

Richard gave a ruby ring to the shrine of Saint Edward to be used in future coronations.[91] He also gave the shrine a full set of vestments, including an elaborate chasuble embroidered with, among other things, the image of Saint Edward and with Edward's arms shown twice. In a letter to the Abbey confirming the gift, he mentions specially that Edward is his predecessor, a role relevant to his own kingship.[92] In his will he follows the formula found in the will of Edward II (died 1327), invoking the Trinity, the Virgin Mary and the whole celestial court, but also adds an invocation to Edward the Confessor and John the Baptist.[93]

SAINT JOHN THE BAPTIST Perhaps the most important of the three saints for Richard was John the Baptist, his patron saint. He is the only saint in the diptych who has any physical contact with the king, presenting him to the Virgin and Child with his hand on the king's back. He holds a lamb in reference to the Lamb of God.

Richard seems to have been supremely devoted to the Baptist. He was born on 6 January, the feast of the Baptism of Christ and acceded to the throne on 22 June, on the eve of the vigil of the feast of the Birth of the Baptist (24 June). Examples of his devotion are numerous. He is shown kneeling before the Baptist in the stained-glass window (Plate 16) in Winchester College, commissioned around 1390 and probably installed in 1393,[94] and the saint almost certainly featured with Richard in a lost altarpiece (see p.58). Indeed one account of the altarpiece says the king was being presented to the Virgin and Child by the

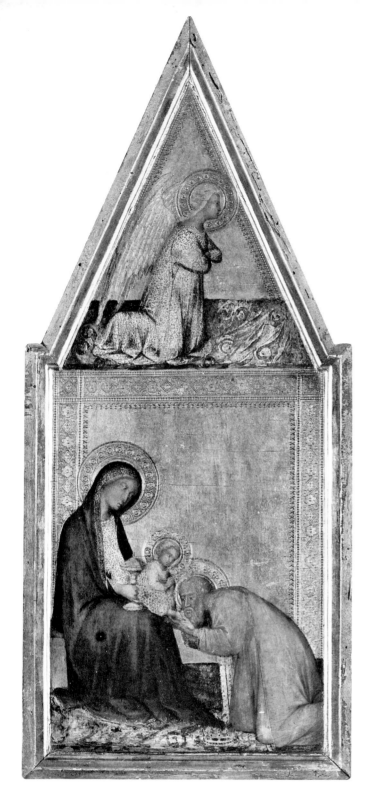
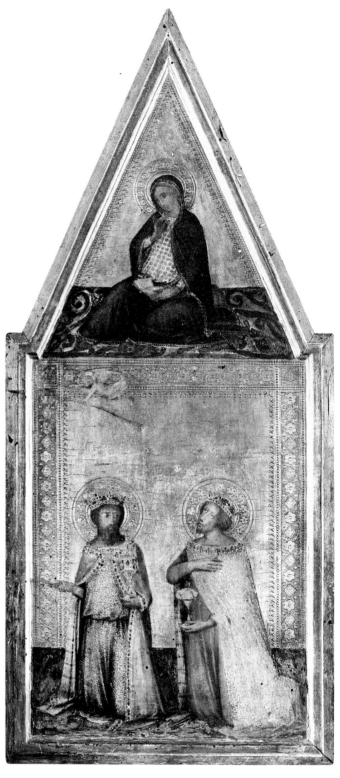

Fig. 17. Naddo Ceccarelli (Sienese painter), *The Adoration of the Magi*, c.1345. Egg tempera on panel, 53 × 22 cm (each panel). Tours, Musée des Beaux-Arts.

Baptist, just as he is in the Wilton Diptych. In 1392 an elaborate reception for the king and queen in the City of London included as its climax at Temple Bar a tableau of John the Baptist in the Wilderness.[95] Among Henry Earl of Derby's New Year gifts to the king in 1398 was a gold tablet with an image of John the Baptist.[96] Richard also acquired relics of the Baptist: in 1386 he received the dish on which the saint's head had lain as a gift from the vicar of All Souls upon

the Pavement, York, and in 1398 he acquired a tooth of the Baptist for which the bearer received a pension of 4 pence a day for life.[97]

On 6 November 1392 the king gave the manor of Aldenham to Westminster Abbey. In return the monks were to celebrate yearly on the king's coronation day a Solemn Mass with music at the altar of Saint John the Baptist for himself and his queen, Anne, during their lifetime and also after their death.[98] The

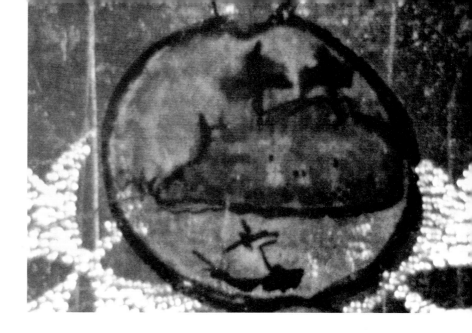

Fig. 18 Infra-red reflectogram of the orb (1 cm wide) at the top of the banner in the Wilton Diptych.

link here of John the Baptist with Richard's coronation day is significant, for each of the three saints represented in the diptych had associations with his kingship; and as we shall see (p.61) they were all three linked to Westminster Abbey, where Richard had been crowned and where the inscription on his tomb specifically invokes John the Baptist.

THE FEAST OF THE EPIPHANY The feast of the Baptism coincides with the feast of Epiphany, or Adoration of the Kings. In medieval paintings of this subject one king is often shown kneeling before the Virgin and Child, while the other two stand or kneel behind (Fig. 17). Similarly, in the left wing of the diptych Richard kneels before the Virgin and Child with Saints Edmund and Edward behind.

It was not uncommon for a patron to be thus identified with one of the Magi.[99] For obvious reasons, the feast of the Epiphany had a special place in the liturgical life of all medieval royal courts. From the time of Edward III at least it was customary for the king to make an oblation of gold, frankincense and myrrh. Richard consistently carried this out, wherever he happened to be, and it is a custom still practised by the British sovereign. Richard's interest in the Magi is linked to the fact that the feast of the Epiphany – 6 January – was also his birthday. The significance of this feast for Richard was almost certainly reinforced by the fact that, according to a contemporary chronicle, when Richard was born in Bordeaux three kings were present – specifically termed 'magi' by the chronicler – the kings of Spain, Navarre and Portugal, who brought Richard precious gifts in the manner of the three Magi.[100]

Richard's preoccupation with the Epiphany is also suggested by the fact that in about 1395 he paid for the enlarging of the crown of one of the kings in the *Adoration of the Magi* in St Stephen's Chapel at Westminster.[101]

England, Angles and Angels

Richard is kneeling in adoration, and yet the position of his hands is strangely ambiguous. They are not closed in prayer, but appear to be open and empty, having just presented something, or having just received something, or, very probably, both. Crucial to the interpretation of the interaction of the figures from one wing to another is the white banner with a red cross held by one of the angels. It appears to refer to the Resurrection (see p.21), but has also been interpreted as the banner of Saint George, patron saint of England. Very likely it represents both ideas. Such doubling up of meaning was not uncommon: in 1419 a lord of Périgord in southern France chose for his device an azure belt with a white shield and red cross 'the better to have in remembrance Our Lord's Passion. And also in honour of Monseigneur St George, so that it may please him ever to succour me well.'[102]

Crowning the very top of the banner in the diptych is an orb. Painted within this orb (Plate 21 and Fig. 18), which measures only one centimetre in diameter, is a tiny map of a green island with trees on the horizon and a small white tower with two turrets and black vertical windows. Above is blue sky, and below is sea, originally made of silver leaf, with a boat in full sail with masts.[103] In the sixteenth century Shakespeare in his play *Richard II* was to write a famous speech, delivered by John of Gaunt, in which he refers to England as 'this little world . . . set in the silver sea' (Act II, Scene 1); whether this is a coincidence or the memory of an actual image is impossible to tell. But the tiny map is a clue to the meaning of the diptych.

In Rome in the seventeenth century there was a large altarpiece, now lost, in which Richard II and his first wife, Anne of Bohemia were shown kneeling before the Virgin. One description says that Richard was offering to her 'the globe or patterne of England', perhaps a globe with a similar representation of England to that in the diptych. The altarpiece, which was probably painted some time between 1382 and 1394, bore the inscription: 'Dos tua Virgo pia haec est; quare rege Maria' (this is your dowry O holy Virgin, therefore rule over it O Mary). It may be that in the Wilton Diptych the tiny map is a symbol of the island of Britain and that Richard is offering England to the Virgin as her dowry. His hands are empty, for he has presumably just presented the banner to the Virgin, who holds her Son. The Christ Child has apparently taken it and passed it to an attendant angel. The Child is now about to bless Richard who will then receive back the banner in a reciprocal gesture of feudal exchange. The boy king is to rule England under the protection, and with the blessing, of the Virgin.

In the same way that the banner has both a religious and a secular significance, so it may be that the angels surrounding the Virgin and Child have a dual role.

Angels are conventionally part of Christian iconography, but it is noticeable that they figure prominently in imagery associated with Richard II. In his procession into London for his coronation figures dressed as angels played a major role, scattering golden leaves and florins before him, offering him cups of wine, while a mechanical angel proffered a crown. Later, in the triumphal procession which marked Richard's reconciliation with the City of London in 1392, angels sang and scattered pieces of gold, a youth and maiden dressed as angels descended from a tower, and there was a tableau of three circles of angels around the Almighty.[104] Angels appear as supporters of the royal arms on the roof of Westmin-

ster Hall, remodelled by Richard II in 1395.[105] And eight angels were to be shown on Richard's tomb along with twelve weeping figures.[106]

There are several problems associated with the angels in the diptych. The first is whether their number is significant. Some writers have said that eleven are depicted in reference to the fact that Richard was in his eleventh year when he acceded to the throne.[107] This seems very plausible in the context of the numerous other references to his accession and kingship, particularly if it was indeed the intention to refer to Richard's coronation in depicting him anachronistically as a young boy.

The angels in the diptych are essentially secular creatures. Although they have wings, they are shown without haloes, and instead wear the more secular chaplets. Listed in the inventories of Richard's possessions are chaplets of roses made of red and white enamel.[108] In the Wilton Diptych the chaplets of red and white roses are more in keeping with the real flowers of the meadow.

The angels are wearing both Richard's personal emblem of the white hart and simple collars of broomcods. It might to the modern mind seem sacrilegious for angels to be shown as Richard's supporters in the heavenly kingdom, but the diptych was not unique in this. Angels carry the badges of Giangaleazzo Visconti, ruler of Milan (died 1402), in a manuscript illumination,[109] and one of the Magi is shown wearing the badge of a gold knot, personal device of Giangaleazzo, in an *Adoration of the Kings* in another Visconti manuscript.[110]

The fusion of religious and secular imagery in the Wilton Diptych – the three kings analogues of the three Magi, the banner alluding both to the Resurrection and to Saint George – raises the question whether the angels might not perhaps be intended to recall the pun, first made by Pope Gregory the Great (c.540–604), when he saw English slave boys in the market in Rome: 'non Angli sed angeli' (not Angles but angels). The angels of the diptych are not only angels but also English and so they wear the livery badges of Richard to show that they support him as their king.

Who Commissioned the Wilton Diptych – and Why?

In the discussion of the imagery in the previous chapters it has been assumed that the Wilton Diptych was commissioned by Richard himself and for his own use. The heraldic evidence suggests that the most likely date for this is after 1395, when Richard first began what amounted to a campaign to use the royal arms impaled with those of Edward the Confessor.[111] This dating is reinforced by the rapprochement between the English and French courts around this time and by Richard's marriage to Isabelle in 1396, before which the use of the broom plant motif is unlikely. However, this is of little help in establishing that Richard himself actually commissioned the painting.

Personal or Posthumous?

A number of writers consider the diptych to have been commissioned by someone other than the king. Some believe it to be a memorial picture, commissioned after the death of Richard,[112] and that it might, for example, have been commissioned by Henry V, when Richard's body was transferred from King's Langley to Westminster Abbey in 1413.[113] This argument is based on an interpretation of the imagery as representing exclusively Richard's reception into heaven, and of the style as being most closely comparable with early fifteenth-century manuscripts (see p.73). However, the miniature scale of the diptych and its essentially portable nature make it inherently unlikely that it is a memorial painting: such a painting would surely have been in a permanent location and on a monumental scale, more along the lines of the portrait of the king enthroned in Westminster Abbey (Plate 26).

Another theory, that it was produced by a secret society or confraternity dedicated to maintaining Richard on the throne,[114] stumbles on the lack of evidence for the existence of any such society. Moreover, the fact that the livery of the white hart was widely distributed among Richard's followers and was therefore not exclusive to any particular group or society would seem to argue against this.[115]

It has also been suggested that the diptych could have been commissioned by Anne of Bohemia or by Isabelle of France – although the latter is less likely given Isabelle's extreme youth – as a birthday gift to Richard, or made as a gift for Isabelle from Richard.[116] However, the heraldic emblems, and the focus of the imagery in the interior scenes, are essentially personal to Richard II, and the emblems on the exterior, where his personal arms and his white hart feature so prominently, seem to signal ownership. It is therefore extremely unlikely that the diptych was commissioned by anyone other than King Richard II himself for his own personal use. What that use was we can make some attempt in the following pages to define more specifically.

The Wilton Diptych as a Crusader Icon

The association of the Wilton Diptych with the alliance with France has led some writers to suggest that it was commissioned by Richard in commemoration of a pledge to undertake a crusade jointly with Charles VI for the recovery of the Holy Land. According to this view the diptych was inspired by the propaganda for the Order of the Passion.[117]

The Order of the Passion was an order of knighthood proposed by the Celestin monk Philippe de Mézières in an illuminated manuscript written in 1395 entitled *Epître au Roi Richart*.[118] In this 'Letter to the King' Mézières also argued the case for Richard's marriage to the French princess, which would create a lasting peace between England and France and enable the two kings to undertake a crusade to the Holy Land. Mézières, one-time Chancellor of Cyprus, had been tutor to Charles VI and continued in his service as his adviser. The manuscript was probably written at the behest of the French king since Charles VI had written a letter to Richard on 15 May 1395 along the same lines after marriage negotiations had begun in February of that year.[119] A second manuscript, *La sustance de la chevalerie de la passion de Iehsu Crist en François*, also written by Philippe de Mézières in 1395, which may have been given to the Earl of Huntingdon, Richard's half brother – one of the twenty English members of the Order – describes in detail the purposes of the Order, the offices of the members, the regulations, the habit to be worn and the arms.[120] The descriptions are accompanied by illuminations.

If the Wilton Diptych does represent Richard II vowing to lead a crusade with Charles VI, this would account for the lavish use of the emblems of the two kings, and in particular the emphasis given to the broomcod, which as we have seen was liberally used by Charles VI[121] and for the 'sacrilege' of showing the angels as retainers, wearing the emblems of both kings. It would also explain the Christian symbolism, in particular the symbols of the Passion – the three nails and crown of thorns – within Christ's halo (Plates 20 and 35), since it was in the Holy Land that Christ suffered death for the redemption of mankind. It is noteworthy that the *Epître* is illuminated with a crown of thorns linking the two crowns of England and France (Plate 17).

But if the diptych is associated with the Order of the Passion, it is surprising that Richard is not shown in the robes of the Order, which were plain blue with a surmantel of white with a red cross, the cross edged with gold in the case of princes (Plate 18). It could be argued that the king, who was fond of fine clothes, would not have felt himself obliged to wear such humble clothing, but the banner in the diptych also differs very considerably from those shown in the manuscript illuminations (Plate 19). The banner of the Order was white with a red cross, a black quatrefoil (to symbolise the Passion of Christ) and a gold lamb, the *Agnus Dei* (to symbolise Christ's Resurrection), both the latter notably absent in the banner in the diptych.[122]

It is crucial to consider whether interpreting the symbol of England in the orb at the top of the banner as the *Dos Mariae* (Dowry of Mary) excludes the crusader theory. Is it still possible to graft on a further layer of meaning and argue that Richard is here dedicating himself, as the King of England entrusted with the Virgin's dowry, to her service in a crusade? In favour of this is the fact that the rules of the Order of the Passion contain the plea to the Virgin to be a 'vierge directrice' to the crusaders, to take the Order under her protection and to plead its cause with her Son.[123] Furthermore, when they met at Ardres in 1396 Richard and Charles are said to have vowed to build a chapel to Our Lady of Peace.[124]

There is one further possible connection with the crusades which also ties in with Richard's preoccupation with the sacred nature of his kingship. It has been suggested[125] that the diptych is linked to the efforts Richard was making towards the end of his reign to have himself re-anointed as king of England with the Holy Oil used at coronations,[126] which had been lost and was found again at the Tower of London in 1399 contained within a golden eagle. According to legend, this phial of oil had been given by the Virgin to Thomas Becket while he was in exile in France with the prophecy that the fifth king of England would recover the Holy Land.[127] In this case it might be possible to interpret the tower in the orb as a symbol of the White Tower, and to argue that Richard is dedicating England to the Virgin in pledge of a crusade to recover the Holy Land. However, this would allow very little time between the discovery of the oil sometime in 1399 and the deposing of Richard in the autumn of that year for the diptych to have been commissioned and executed.

Coronation and Salvation

The evident emphasis on Richard's kingship has led some earlier writers to see the Wilton Diptych as commemorating events which established that kingship. One possibility which has been put forward is that it commemorates Richard's visit to Westminster before riding out to confront the rebels massed under Wat Tyler at Smithfield in 1381. In favour of this theory is Richard's youthful appearance in the diptych – he was aged only fourteen when he met the rebels – and the fact that he dedicated himself to the Virgin before riding out.[128] It was an act of courageous leadership and assertion of his own authority which he could well have wished to remember.

It has also been suggested that the diptych was commissioned to commemorate the king's coronation.[129] Again the king's youthful appearance and the overt allusions to his kingship and the coronation make this a plausible theory. However, the Wilton Diptych is not so much a commemoration of one particular event as a visual expression of an idea – the idea of kingship. There are numerous occasions during his reign when Richard might have wished to celebrate his kingship. But the period which ties in with the chronology suggested by the heraldic evidence is 1397. Having made peace with France, Richard turned to home and acted to assert his absolute authority. He arrested the three Appellants who had earlier undermined his supremacy (see pp.17ff.), the Duke of Gloucester, and the Earls of Arundel and Warwick, and all those who had criticised him. Gloucester fortuitously died, Arundel was beheaded, and Warwick was pardoned. Richard rewarded those faithful to him and members of Parliament had to swear an oath of loyalty at the shrine of Edward the Confessor. Richard felt himself to be 'entier emperour de son Roialme d'Engleterre' (absolute emperor of his kingdom of England).[130] It would have been a fitting moment to commission for his private use an elaborate testimony to his kingship.

This theory may perhaps be taken one step further. As we have seen, the Wilton Diptych is the visual expression of a complex intermingling of the sacred and the secular, of religious devotion and the idea of kingship. The building which embodied these concepts was Westminster Abbey – the building in which Richard was crowned and in which he intended to be buried.

The Abbey functioned as both shrine and mausoleum for the English kings, and particularly for Richard II.[131] His interest in the Abbey is well documented: he contributed towards the building of the nave[132] and the northern porch was built during his reign.[133] He worshipped there in times of crisis. The *Liber Regalis*,[134] which is still in the Abbey, may well have been made for him. He gave it many gifts, including two banners of Saint Edmund and one of Saint Edward. He also gave the shrine of Saint Edward in 1389 a complete set of vestments, which included a chasuble embroidered on one side with the Trinity, the Virgin, Saints Edward the Confessor and Edmund, and the arms of Edward, Richard and Anne; on the other side were the Virgin, Saint John the Baptist, the arms of a certain abbess and again the arms of Edward, Richard and Anne.[135] Precisely these saints are shown in the Wilton Diptych. Furthermore, these three saints had neighbouring chapels dedicated to them across the east end of Westminster Abbey (Fig. 19), and aligned in precisely the order in which they are shown in the diptych:[136] Edmund (south), Edward (centre) and John the Baptist (north). Richard planned to have his tomb in the midst of this sequence, close to the shrine of the Confessor.

Richard commissioned his tomb – with effigies of himself and Anne of Bohemia (see Figs. 2 and 5) – in April 1395, nearly a year after Anne's death in June 1394. The robes in his effigy are pounced with the white hart and broomcod (Fig. 12) – the very same emblems found in the Wilton Diptych – with the addition of the sunburst, also one of Richard's emblems. The royal arms impaled with the arms of Edward the Confessor decorate the canopy above his head (see Fig. 16). Above all, the tomb bears an inscription calling upon Christ to save Richard through the intercession of the Baptist who in the diptych *presents him* (my italics) to the Virgin: 'O clemens Christe – cui devotus fuit iste; Votis Baptiste salves quem pretulit iste' (O merciful Christ to whom he [Richard] was devoted, save him through the prayers of the Baptist who presented him).[137]

At around this same time, Richard was probably

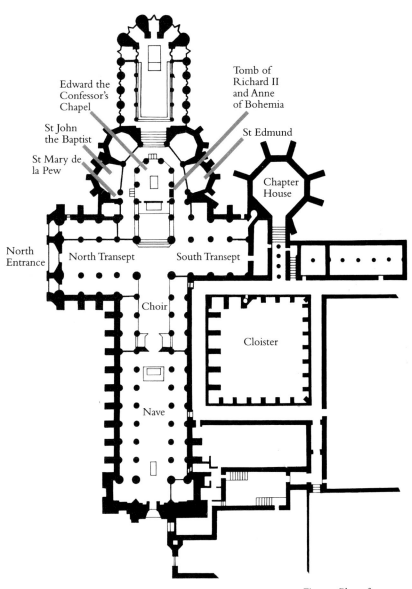

Fig. 19 Plan of Westminster Abbey showing the alignment of the chapels of John the Baptist, Edward the Confessor and Edmund.

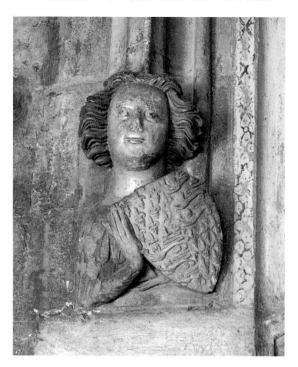 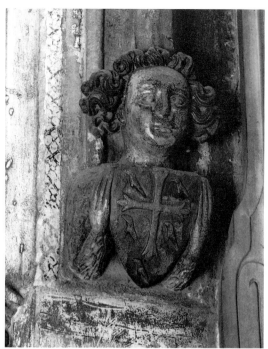

Fig. 20 Angels at the entrance to the chapel of St Mary de la Pew holding the royal arms (left) and the arms of Edward the Confessor (right). London, Westminster Abbey.

involved with another commission: the portrait of himself enthroned (Plate 26) which hangs in Westminster Abbey and which may date from around 1395.[138] The tomb monuments refer to his death and future salvation, and the painting to his kingship, and all these themes are united in the Wilton Diptych.

The link between the diptych and Westminster Abbey can be taken one step further. Immediately adjacent to the chapel of St John the Baptist, and now opening onto it,[139] is a tiny chapel, once known as the chapel of St Erasmus, and before that as St Mary de la Pew (it is now called Our Lady of the Pew).[140] This chapel dates back at least to the latter half of the fourteenth century: on the right wall above the altar is painted a white hart, gorged and couchant; at the entrance to the chapel are sculpted two half-length angels, the one on the right holding the arms of Edward the Confessor, and the one on the left holding the royal arms of England and France ancient (Fig. 20). This heraldic combination suggests that the chapel was used by Richard II as his oratory for private devotion, as opposed to the ceremonial occasions when he sat in the choir of the Abbey.

The chapel probably always had a Marian dedication, even if not the present dedication of St Mary de la Pew, since the roof boss is an Assumptive Virgin, and the altar niche may orginally have housed a statue of the Virgin.[141] Its wide ledge, about 73 cm across, could well have accommodated the open diptych with its appropriate imagery of the Virgin with Saints

Edmund, Edward and John the Baptist. It is possible therefore that Richard II commissioned the Wilton Diptych for use in the chapel when he went there to worship privately.

The scale of the diptych and its deliberately portable nature mean that it could also have been used by Richard in his own royal chapels. He had an oratory in the Palace of Westminster, probably identifiable with the chapel confusingly also called St Mary de la Pew[142] – the same name as the small chapel in Westminster Abbey discussed above – and the Wilton Diptych could have been commissioned for use there too.[143]

Richard also had chapels at his various palaces at Sheen, King's Langley,[144] Eltham,[145] and Ireland.[146] Indeed one suggestion is that the diptych was specifically painted to take to Ireland.[147]

We know from the accounts of the Great Wardrobe of 1385 that when Richard travelled to Scotland he commissioned what seems to be either a portable altar or altarpiece.[148] If it was a portable altarpiece, it may have been a predecessor of the Wilton Diptych which became obsolete when Richard acquired a new set of heraldic emblems following his marriage to Isabelle of France. This is of course speculation. What is certain is that wherever Richard took the Wilton Diptych, he would have had a constant reminder of the sacred nature of his kingship and of the Abbey where he had been crowned and where he intended to be buried.

NOTES

1. See notes 64 and 74 below.

2. See Wilkins 1969, p.166, for rose chaplets.

3. I am extremely grateful to John Harvey and Celia Fisher for helping to identify the flowers in the diptych, not all of which are botanically accurate.

4. See Levi d'Ancona 1977, pp.332ff. for roses and the Virgin, and p.187 for irises.

5. Palgrave 1836, III, p.332, items 114, 115, 154; p.348, item 250.

6. *The Westminster Chronicle*, p.42.

7. Stow 1977, p.166. In fact, disinterment of the king's body in 1871, if indeed the body in the tomb was his, showed him to have been extremely tall with an exceptionally small skull (Stanley, *Archaeologia*, 1880, pp.309–25). Richard's body was displayed in London, covered in lead, after his death and then buried in King's Langley (see St John Hope, *Archaeologia*, 1907, pp.517–70), although not in the tomb in King's Langley which Richard had intended for himself before he changed his mind and decided to be buried in Westminster Abbey (see Powell, *History Today*, 1965, pp.713–18). His body was moved in 1413 to the tomb he had commissioned for himself in Westminster Abbey.

8. Whittingham, BM, 1971, pp.12–21 *passim*.

9. The contract is PRO, E 101/473/7. In April 1395 Richard was in Ireland and it has been argued (Whittingham, BM, 1971, p.12) that the pattern must therefore date from before 1394 when he left for Ireland. However, the head in the tomb effigy was in fact cast separately (Plenderleith and Maryon, *The Antiquaries Journal*, 1959, p.90), which suggests that it was made separately, and therefore the only definite date for it is the completion date of 1398. The casting must have been complete by 7 December 1398 when additional payments suggest that the gilding was begun, probably being complete by 14 April 1399 (Harvey, *Archaeologia*, 1961, p.8, n.6). In *Age of Chivalry*, Cat. 446, the likely suggestion is made that the design had been drawn up by someone other than the mason and coppersmith; in view of the similarities of the patterns on the robe with the Wilton Diptych, the painter of the diptych cannot be excluded as the designer.

10. e.g. Tristram, *The Month*, 1949, II, p.383.

11. Beard, *Connoisseur*, 1931, p.375, argued that the idealisation was in order to minimise the difference in age between Richard and his child bride Isabelle, an idea taken up by Whittingham (BM, 1971, p.20).

12. Nichols 1780, pp.191–202, esp. p.191.

13. Eagles were included in the arms of Bohemia. They also decorated the coronation robes (see Tristram, *The Month*, 1949, I, p.384).

14. Richard also used the badge of ostrich feathers of his father early in his reign – see Nicolas, *Archaeologia*, XXXI, 1846, pp.350–84. The sword which Richard gave to the City of Lincoln, probably at his visit in 1386, has ostrich feathers engraved on the pommel, as well as the royal arms. The scabbard, which is modern, is decorated with silver white harts, and sunbursts, probably reflecting the design of the original. I am grateful to the Mayor of the City of Lincoln for allowing me to examine this sword.

15. Riley 1868, pp.429 and 443.

16. Clarke, BM, 1931, p.287.

17. Paley Baildon, *Archaeologia*, 1911, p.511. The documents came from a private muniment room in the Midlands (location not given). They are likely to be from the king's accounts since they contain payments for mending a collar of the queen.

18. Müller and Steingräber, *Münchener Jahrbuch der Bildenden Kunst*, 1954, pp.29–79. See also Lightbown 1992, p.158.

19. It was found on the site of the Dominican Priory of Dunstable. *Age of Chivalry*, Cat. 659. Cherry, *The Journal of the British Archaeological Association*, 1969, pp.38–53. See also Lightbown 1992, pp.157ff. and 166ff.

20. Palgrave 1836, III, p.356, item 327.

21. One of the emblems of Charles VI was the *cerf volant* (a winged hart) said to have been adopted by the French king in 1382. See Beaune 1981, pp.128ff. For a discussion of the relationship between the winged hart and the white hart of Richard II see Bath 1979, pp.25–42 (typescript in the National Gallery archives). For the rivalry between the royal houses of England and France expressed in the adoption of emblems see Lightbown 1992, p.166.

22. Calendar of the Close Rolls preserved in the Public Record Office, Richard II, vol. VI, AD 1396–9, London, 1927, p.210; letter of 20 August 1397 from Woodstock.

23. Perroy 1933, p.103, no.152.

24. Wylie 1884, I, p.69.

25. See Wylie 1898, IV, p.161.

26. See John of Gaunt's will published by Nichols 1780, p.157.

27. Dehaisnes 1866, pp.865–6. This was probably the same jewel recorded in the possession of the Duke of Burgundy in 1435. See *Age of Chivalry*, p.524 under Cat. 725.

28. *Age of Chivalry*, Cat. 725.

29. Spencer 1990, pp.97ff.

30. *Age of Chivalry*, Cat. 448.

31. Day and Steele 1936, II, lines 35–9 and 41–3; and Wright 1859, I, pp.379–82.

32. Clarke, BM, 1931, p.287. In 1387–8 two pieces of plate engraved with a hart were among chattels forfeited by Richard. Listed in the royal possessions inventoried in 1400 are numerous articles decorated with the white hart (Palgrave 1836, III, pp.313ff.).

33. *Age of Chivalry*, Cat. 724 and 726.

34. For Cambridge, Trinity Hall MS 17 see Cronin 1921. The text dates from around 1395. See Robinson 1988, p.107, no.394.

35. Harvey, *Archaeologia*, 1961, p.7.

36. In 1386 Richard ordered robes of blue velvet and red velvet embroidered with white harts for the feast of the Purification of the Virgin (PRO, E 101/401/16, Livery Roll of 1385–8). I am extremely grateful to Lisa Monnas for this unpublished reference.

37. Among the many red wax seals appended to the contract for the king's tomb (see note 9) is a seal with the white hart.

38. See *Age of Chivalry*, Cat. 692. Pamela Tudor-Craig has pointed out to me that plaster casts of two of the corbels with the white harts are in the Sir John Soane Museum, London.

39. Stanley 1869, pp.148–9.

40. A gift of 100 marks made to York Minster in 1395 was acknowledged by the carving of a chained hart on a capital above the entry to the south choir aisle. Harvey in *Essays McKisack*, 1971, p.207. Richard also presented a relic of one of the Holy Innocents in a silver and gilt shrine; see Aylmer and Cant 1977, p.165.

41. Painted by Thomas Lytlington with white harts with gilt antlers. See Harvey, *Archaeologia*, 1961, p.7.

42. Tanner 1948, Plates 46 and 47; also Eames 1977, p.249.

43. Harvey, *Archaeologia*, 1961, p.17.

44. The royal palace at Eltham had hall windows decorated with harts made by Geoffrey Glasyer in 1396–7 (Harvey, *Archaeologia*, 1961, p.7).

45. CPR for 7 April 1395. The brass is published in Cotman 1839, I, Plate XV, opp. p.13. The brass was placed there after the death in 1416 of his first wife, a kinswoman and maid of honour to Anne of Bohemia. Sir Simon himself was eventually buried in Norwich in the church of Friars Preachers. He is shown wearing the Order of the Garter which he received in the first year of the reign of Henry V.

46. Harvey, *Archaeologia*, 1961, p.16.

47. For a discussion of broomcod collars see Clarke, BM, 1931, pp.287ff. For the Arundel incident see Clarke, op.cit., p.289. For the use of collars see Lightbown 1992, pp.246ff. He gives the date of the Arundel incident as 1393. An example of the collar of linked Ss of the Lancastrians is in the Museum of London.

48. The key articles were written by Nichols in *Archaeologia*, 1842, pp.32–59, and *The Gentleman's Magazine*, 1842, I, pp.157–61; II, pp.250–8; III, pp.378–9. The most recent study of broomcod collars is by Lightbown 1992, pp.268ff.

49. Nichols, *The Gentleman's Magazine*, 1842, II, pp.251ff.

50. For the use of the broomcod at the French court see Boulton 1987, pp.428–9.

51. See Nichols, *The Gentleman's Magazine*, 1842, II, p.256, and Guiffrey, *Bibliothèque de l'Ecole des Chartes*, 1887, XLVIII, pp.74, 75, 77, and Boulton 1987, pp.428–9.

52. Some fragments are also in the Bargello Museum, Florence; see Monnas, CIETA *Bulletin*, 1986, p.72.

53. Charles VI and his courtiers are wearing simple broomcod collars in a Parisian manuscript illumination executed *c.*1403–4 showing Christine de Pisan presenting her work to the French king, now in Brussels, Bibliothèque Royale (MS 10983,f.1; see Gaspar and Lyna 1937, Pl.CI b), and two courtiers are shown wearing them in a book of *Poésies* by Christine de Pisan (Paris, Bibliothèque Nationale, MS fr.836). In a manuscript of 1412 (Geneva, Bibliothèque publique et universitaire, f.163, ff.4 and 7) Charles VI is shown wearing yet two further types of collar, one of linked flowers with white pearls and a pod with pearls at the shoulder, and one of linked flowers with a pair of pendant pods in front (Sterling 1987, Figs. 254 and 255).

54. The illumination showing Charles VI opens the second volume of Harley MS 4431 in the British Library. The first volume shows Christine de Pisan presenting her work to Isabeau de Bavière, wife of Charles. The manuscript was attributed by Meiss to the Master of Christine de Pisan's *Cité des Dames* and his workshop, *c.*1405–10 (Meiss 1974, pp.39 and 292, and Sterling 1987, pp.287ff.).

55. For example in an inventory of 4 December 1408 made at Blois of the possessions of the Duke and Duchess of Orléans. See Graves 1926, pp.86ff., items 237 and 238; p.106, item 420; p.109, item 462.

56. Boulton 1987, pp.428–9.

57. The collar made for Charles was composed of two gold rolls with between them double broompods; around the collar on the cods were nine bars (potences), each surrounded by pearls, and in the intervals between them hung fifty gold letters making the (French) king's motto JAMES (*jamais* = never) ten times over. A ruby was set at the front of the collar, encircled by pearls, and at the back were two open broomcods of gold, one enamelled white and the other green, and within each one were three large pearls. In addition the gold rolls were stippled with the branches, flowers and pods of the broom plant. This description comes in the accounts of Charles Poupart, jeweller to Charles VI, for the various objects made for the wedding celebrations of Isabelle, which took place by proxy in the Sainte-Chapelle in Paris. They included robes, crowns, hats, belts, clasps, jewels, gold plate, tapestries, linen – and dolls – *etc.* ordered by the king for Isabelle and the Dukes of Berry, Burgundy, Orléans and Bourbon. As well as broomcod collars for the French king and for Richard, there was one for each of Richard's three uncles. The relevant volume of the accounts in the Chambre des Comptes was copied, and survives as Paris, Bibliothèque Nationale, MS fr. 20684, f.465. The text was transcribed by Helyot 1719, VIII, p.278, who gave the date as 1393, and by Mirot 1902, XXIX, pp.151–2, who gave the date as 1398.

The descriptions of the collars were published by

Clarke (BM, 1931, p.288). The manuscript was checked on behalf of Harvey (*Archaeologia*, 1961, p.9, n.1) by Jean Chazelas in 1957 (typescript in the National Gallery archives), who established the date of the gift as 1396. The accounts of 1397 included mention of a repair to a collar which was similar to that which the king had sent to the king of England, making it certain that the gift took place before 1397. The date of 1398 given by Mirot (see above) may be explained by the fact that this was the date of account (quittance). The date for the gift of broomcod collars is given as 1393 by Lightbown (1992, p.269) but with no accompanying reference.

58. It was extremely common for the collars belonging to the French royal family to have the pods enamelled in green and white, see Graves 1926, p.86, item 238; p.106, item 420.

59. One of Isabelle's collars consisted of gold, with eight open broom flowers, four with rubies at the centre, and eight open broomcods, each with six pearls within and a fastening hanging in front with a ruby, a sapphire and pearls around it; another was of broomcods enamelled with white, with a pair of pendant broomcods (Mirot 1902, pp.130 and 141).

60. Palmer, *Bulletin of the Institute of Historical Research*, 1971, pp.1–17.

61. See Meyer 1881, pp.212–13. Meyer transcribes an account of the meeting from MS 46, ff.104–6, in Oriel College Oxford. Cited by Clarke, BM, 1931, p.288, n.34; and Harvey, *Archaeologia*, 1961, p.10, n.5.

62. See Harvey, *Archaeologia*, 1961, p.7 and n.3.

63. Henry of Lancaster, Earl of Derby, took over the white swan of the de Bohun family when he married Mary de Bohun. See *Age of Chivalry*, p.488.

64. Meyer 1881, p.217. The collar was worth 5,000 marks. A collar of rosemary described as the livery of the dead queen is itemised in the royal possessions in 1400 (Palgrave 1836, III, p.357, item 334). See also note 74.

65. See Harvey, *Archaeologia*, 1961, pp.8–9. This has been firmly denied by Nichols in *The Gentleman's Magazine*, 1842, II, p.257. The name Plantagenet was derived originally from the nickname given to Geoffrey, Count of Anjou, father of Henry II, who wore a sprig of broom in his cap. It was only first formally used as a surname in 1460 when Richard, Duke of York, wanted to assert his superiority over the Lancastrian line (see *Dictionary of National Biography*, vol. XV).

66. The pouncing or stippling was carried out after the gilding, which was probably done between 7 December 1398 and 14 April 1399 when a further £300 additional to the other payments was made (see also note 9). For the tomb contract see *Age of Chivalry*, Cat. 446.

67. See the letter from James G. Mann, BM, LIX, July–Dec. 1931, p.100.

68. Tout 1928, IV, p.345.

69. Palgrave 1836, III, p.313.

70. *Age of Chivalry*, Cat. 697.

71. Palgrave 1836, III, p.354, item 307, and p.357, items 332 and 333.

72. Palgrave 1836, III, p.354, item 307, and p.357, items 332 and 333.

73. Richard commissioned two collars of unspecified design in 1394 (see Devon 1837, p.253).

74. Douët d'Arcq 1864, II, p.275. An inventory of 1400 describes a collar of rosemary as livery of Queen Anne (Wylie 1898, IV, p.196). Ostriches decorate Anne's robes on her tomb effigy. See also note 64.

75. Froissart (ed. Kervyn de Lettenhove 1872, vol. XVI, p.205); cited by Lightbown 1992, p.270, et al.

76. Harvey, *Archaeologia*, 1961, p.8.

77. Lightbown 1992, p.270, considers this to have been because of English claims to the French throne.

78. Spencer 1990, pp.98ff.

79. Spencer 1990, p.48–9.

80. Tanner, *Journal of the British Archaeological Association*, 1952, p.3.

81. Wickham Legg, *Archaeologia*, 1890, p.227.

82. Galbraith 1927, pp.111 and 114; and *The Westminster Chronicle*, p.415.

83. Wickham Legg, *Archaeologia*, 1890, pp.199 and 223.

84. See Spencer 1990, pp.49–51.

85. Tanner, *Journal of the British Archaeological Association*, 1952, pp.1–12.

86. For example, in the stained glass of St Mary, Westwell. See Griffin, *Archaeologia Cantiana*, 1935, pp.170–6.

87. *The Westminster Chronicle*, p.451.

88. Tanner, *Journal of the British Archaeological Association*, 1952, p.3.

89. Wickham Legg, 1901, p.xliv.

90. Wickham Legg 1901, pp.106–7 and 127. He gives a full transcription and translation of the *Liber Regalis*.

91. Wickham Legg, *Archaeologia*, 1890, p.282. This was to remain in the king's custody, unless he were out of England. The rest of the regalia were in the custody of the abbot at Westminster Abbey.

92. Wickham Legg, *Archaeologia*, 1890, p.280.

93. Nichols 1780, p.59, for the will of Edward II, and p.191 for the will of Richard II.

94. *Age of Chivalry*, Cat. 613. The glass was made by Thomas of Oxford and his workshop. A watercolour of 1802 shows the window before it was dismantled in 1821 (Harvey and King, *Archaeologia*, 1971, pp.149–77, esp. Pl.LXXI). The College was built by William of Wykeham who was represented in the adjacent glass kneeling before the Virgin and Child (*Age of Chivalry*, Cat. 612). Building of the College began in 1387; there were at least two royal visits (25 July and 16 and 17 September 1393). See Harvey, letter in *The Month*, 1949, II, pp.433ff., and *The Month*, 1950, p.236.

95. See the description by the Carmelite friar Richard Maidstone in Wright 1859, pp.294–5, and Barron in *Essays McKisack*, 1971, pp.190ff.

96. PRO, DL 28/1/6. Account book of William

Loveney, Keeper of the Wardrobe of the Earl of Derby, 1 Feb. 1397 – 1 Feb. 1398. I owe this reference to Caroline Barron.

97. CPR, Richard II, 1385–9, p.194, and 1396–9, p.329.

98. Bliss and Twemlow 1902, p.430.

99. Kirsch 1991, p.36, n.79, cites comparable examples, one of which is contemporary with the diptych: the Boucicaut Hours (Paris, Musée Jacquemart André, MS 2, f.83v) of *c.*1405–8; this shows one of the Magi wearing a collar of knotted twigs, emblem of Maréchal Boucicaut's friend, Louis d'Orléans, assassinated in 1407 (see Sterling 1987, Fig. 246; he dates the manuscript *c.* 1410–12). See also Beaune 1981, Plate 3, for Charles VII of France depicted as one of the Magi in the Hours of Etienne Chevalier attributed to Jean Fouquet, 1452–61.

100. *Chronica W. Thorn. mon. S. Augustini Cantuariae,* in *Historia Anglicanae Scriptores X* (ed. Twysden), 1652, col.2142. Cited by Thurston, *The Month,* CLIV, 1929, p.31, who suggests it was apocryphal but probably well known. I am grateful to Shelagh Mitchell for the information concerning Richard's oblations on the feast of the Epiphany which she is to publish in a forthcoming paper.

101. Mathew 1968, pp.12ff., and p.180, n.5.

102. Lightbown 1992, p.254.

103. See Gordon, BM, CXXXIV, 1992, pp.662–7. This map seems to be entirely different from the symbols of the created world found for example in the Westminster Retable (Binski, *Journal of the British Archaeological Association,* 1987, pp.160, 168 and Pl.XXXVII B), or in the Hours of Jean de Navarre in *The Trinity* (Paris, Bibliothèque Nationale, n.a.lat.3145, f.11; see Sterling 1987, pp.105ff. and Fig. 53); or in the Bedford Hours and Psalter (London, British Library, Additional MS 42131, f.226).

104. See Kipling in *Pageantry in the Shakespearean Theater,* 1985, pp.83–103, esp. pp.86 and 88.

105. *Age of Chivalry,* Cat. 445. This was copied by Richard's half brother, Thomas Holland, Duke of Exeter, at Dartington Hall in Devon, where his arms have angel supporters.

106. Rymer, *Foedera,* London 1728, VII, p.797.

107. See the typescript of notes from Everard Green dated 17 March 1905 in the National Gallery archives; also Thurston, *The Month,* 1929, p.31; Tristram, *The Month,* 1949, p.385.

108. Palgrave 1836, III, p.356, item 326.

109. See Davies 1957, p.95.

110. Kirsch 1991, p.36. The manuscript is Paris, Bibliothèque Nationale, lat.757, f.293v.

111. Harvey, *Archaeologia,* 1961, pp.5ff.

112. Shaw, BM, 1934, pp.175–81; Panofsky 1953, p.118; Galbraith 1942, pp.237ff.; Wormald, JWCI, 1954, p.202; Alexander 1983, p.146. Galway's interpretation of the diptych as a memorial to Joan of Kent, commissioned by Richard's half sister, the Countess of St Pol, *c.*1390–2, based on the supposed resemblance of the Virgin to Joan of Kent, and of

the Christ Child to Edward of Angoulême handing his inheritance to his brother, seems to enter the realm of pure fantasy (see Galway, *Archaeological Journal,* 1952, pp.9–14).

113. Davies 1957, p.100, n.11, points out that Henry V, reputedly in atonement for the deposition, founded three monasteries.

114. Harvey, *Archaeologia,* 1961, pp.5–6.

115. The wide distribution also led Anstis to conclude that one could not argue that the diptych was connected in any way with the Order of the Garter (Anstis 1724, I, p.112).

116. For example, Whittingham, GBA, p.147. Beard, *The Connoisseur,* 1931, p.375, suggested that it might have been given to Charles VI for Isabelle when the two kings met in October 1396. The theory that it was a gift from Isabelle was discounted by Clarke, BM, 1931, p.290, who argued that all the things Isabelle brought from France were documented. The intriguing possibility remains that the diptych was commissioned by Richard as a birthday gift for himself. The references to his birthday on the feast of the Epiphany are clearly implicit in the compositional allusions to the three Magi and in the presence of John the Baptist, his patron saint. Moreover, one of the few books known to have been made specially for Richard himself includes one passage which classifies kings according to their gifts to themselves as well as to others (see Taylor, *Proceedings of the Leeds Philosophical and Literary Society,* 1971, pp.194ff.).

117. Originally suggested by Scharf 1882, pp.65ff. His theory was expanded by Clarke, BM, 1931, pp.283ff., and then taken up by Tristram, *The Month,* 1949, I, p.390, who considered it a possible minor secondary theme; it was reiterated as the main theme by Palmer 1972, pp.205 and 242–4, and also by Tyerman 1988, p.297.

118. London, British Library, Royal MS B.VI. Trans. and ed. Coopland 1975.

119. Palmer, *Bulletin of the Institute of Historical Research,* 1971, pp.1–17.

120. Oxford, Bodleian Library, MS Ashmole 813. See Clarke, BM, 1931, p.293. The members are listed in another manuscript in French (Paris, Arsenal MS 2251, ff.113b–114a); see Clarke, loc. cit., n.56.

121. A lost work showed Charles VI in the company of his wife kneeling before a golden image of the Virgin, and two aspects of this work were similar to the Wilton Diptych: a broomcod collar which was worn by a herald standing behind Charles, and the arms of Saint George on the herald's clothes. The lost work was at Ingolstadt. See Nichols, *The Gentleman's Magazine,* 1942, II, p.256, for a full description.

122. The only banner similar to that in the diptych is the minute one held by the lamb, and it seems unlikely that this would have been the detail singled out by the painter of the Wilton Diptych to represent the banner of the Order. Clarke (BM, 1931, p.294)

argued that the discrepancies in the various depictions of the banner and in the written description are attributable to the fact that the exact design had not yet been determined.

123. Oxford, Bodleian Library, MS Ashmole 813, ff.17 and 18.

124. See Walsingham's *Historia Anglicana* in Riley 1864, p.221; also Meyer 1881, p.215, and Davies 1957, p.99, n.7.

125. Tristram, *The Month*, 1949, I, p.388.

126. The story was spread that Henry IV had been anointed with this oil in yet another attempt to legitimise his succession. See Walsingham's *Historia Anglicana* in Riley 1864, p.239.

127. See Wickham Legg 1901, pp.69ff.

128. Suggested by Cust 1909, pp.16–19; also Borenius and Tristram 1927, pp.27–8. According to Froissart he dedicated himself to a statue of the Virgin: 'et s'en vint à Westmoustier et oy messe en l'église, et tout li signeur avoecques luy. En celle église a une ymage de Nostre-Dame à une petite cappelle, qui fait grans miracles et grans vertus, et en laquelle li roi d'Engletierre ont tousjours eu grant confiance et créance, et se offri à luy et puis monta à cheval' (Kervyn de Lettenhove 1869, IX, p.409). Froissart seems to be talking about Westminster Abbey. However, the statue he mentions was almost certainly that in the Chapel of St Mary de la Pew in Westminster Palace, although there may also have been a statue of the Virgin in a small oratory in the Abbey used by Richard II. See also Galbraith 1927, p.146, and Stow 1977, p.65, and *The Westminster Chronicle*, pp.8–10.

129. Borenius and Tristram 1927, pp.27–8. Evans (*Archaeological Journal*, 1950, p.5) suggested that it was to commemorate Richard's second coronation in St Stephen's Chapel in 1389. Tristram himself took up the theme again arguing that it was a votive picture painted on the occasion of the coronation in 1377 (*The Month*, 1949, I, pp.379–90). This ignores the heraldic evidence for dating produced by Clarke (BM, 1931, pp.283ff.), but much of his analysis remains valid. It was also thought to commemorate the coronation by Mathew (1968, pp.199ff.).

130. *Rotuli Parliamentorum*, vol. III, p.343. For events of 1397 see Duls 1975, pp.71ff., and Steel 1941, p.240.

131. I am grateful to Nigel Saul for allowing me to see the typescript of his forthcoming article 'Richard II and Westminster Abbey'. Richard's original intention seems to have been to be buried in King's Langley (see Powell 1965, pp.713ff.).

132. Rackham, *Proceedings of the British Academy*, IV, 1909–10, pp.40ff.

133. Stanley 1869, pp.148–9.

134. For the *Liber Regalis* and its dating see Binski on Westminster Abbey and the Plantagenets, forthcoming.

135. Wickham Legg, *Archaeologia*, 1890, pp.227 and 280.

See also Clarke, BM, 1931, p.283; and Walcott 1873, pp.325, 328; Harvey, *Archaeologia*, 1961, p.5 and n.7, and Barron in *Essays McKisack*, 1971, p.195.

136. A point first made by Wormald, JWCI, 1954, p.200.

137. The whole inscription is given in *Royal Commission on Historical Monuments*, 1924, p.31.

138. Payments made in an issue roll of 15 December 1395 (PRO, E.403/554) include payments for 'the picture of an image in the likeness of the king in the choir of the church' which have been thought to refer to the Westminster Abbey portrait (*Age of Chivalry*, Cat. 713. Under this entry Tudor Craig points out that the tomb and portrait were probably commissioned at the same time as the Wilton Diptych). Selby Whittingham (BM, 1971, p.20, n.52) considered the payment was more likely to have been for painting a statue. Paul Binski has suggested to me that the portrait could have come from Westminster Palace.

139. The piercing dates from the early sixteenth century. See *Royal Commission on Historical Monuments*, 1924, p.73.

140. Micklethwaite, *Archaeologia*, 1873, pp.93–9.

141. The present statue is modern.

142. See Kingsford, *Archaeologia*, 1917, pp.1–20.

143. Conway, BM, 1929, pp.36–45. He was following a suggestion first made by Everard Green (typescript dated 17 March 1905 in the National Gallery archives).

144. In Michaelmas 1396 Richard donated a missal and chalice to the chapel there (Devon 1837, p.263).

145. On 6 July 1382 Richard paid for a bell for the chapel there (Devon 1837, p.247).

146. See Devon 1837, p.281, for payments to a certain Henry Dryhurst bringing from Ireland 'the furniture of a chapel and ornaments of same, which formerly belonged to the late King Richard the Second' (5 March 1401).

147. Evans, *Archaeological Journal*, 1950, p.4. Tudor Craig in *Age of Chivalry*, p.135.

148. PRO, E.101/401/5: Et pro merem tabul ac pro gemell hokes et anul de fer ac per factur unius altar portatil ordin ad carrand eum domino rege contra viag suum ad partes Scoc. 17s 4d. (And for the timber for a panel and for two identical hooks and rings of iron and for the making of a portable altar (or altarpiece?) ordered for carrying with the lord king for his voyage to Scotland). It may be significant that this payment follows on a number of payments to Gilbert Prince. The need for hooks and rings suggests the possibility that the payments are not for a portable altar but for a portable altarpiece consisting of two panels hinged together with iron rings and with hooks for closing – i.e. the predecessor of the Wilton Diptych. I am grateful to Lisa Monnas for her help in transcribing this passage.

THE MAKING OF THE WILTON DIPTYCH

The Artist and his Background

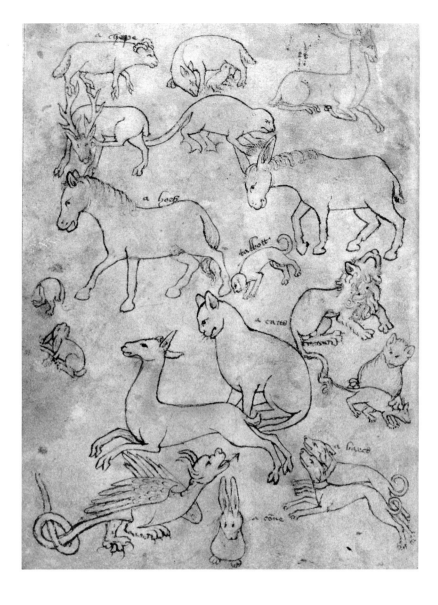

Fig. 21 Studies of animals including two harts, one seated, one scratching its ear, by an unknown English artist of the late 14th century. Cambridge, Magdalene College, MS Pepsyian 1916, f.9b.

Who could have devised the complex interplay of ideas which make the Wilton Diptych so intriguing? Was it the king? Was it the painter? Or was it a collaboration of minds? No contemporary documents have come to light which mention the artist or the commission. Nor is there any comparable work among panel paintings or manuscript illuminations in England, or abroad, which can be attributed to the same artist or even the same workshop. Due partly to the iconoclasm of the Reformation period and the purges under Oliver Cromwell, very little English panel painting survives from the Middle Ages, and what does survive is largely provincial and comparatively coarse.

The panel paintings and manuscript illuminations which survive from the courts of Europe towards the end of the fourteenth century are characterised by a refined style which combines an interest in the natural world of plants and animals (see for example Fig. 21) with attention to decorative effects, exploited in the rendering of rich fabrics, jewels and elaborate architecture. It is a type of painting fashionable among the courts of Europe which has been called 'International Gothic'. The Wilton Diptych is perhaps the outstanding example of this style. The hauntingly beautiful image of the white hart on the exterior, naturalistic in all but its antlers, which are not painted but stippled in the gold, creates a tantalising dichotomy between reality and artificiality. On the interior the rich surface effects of the robes and jewels are combined with naturalistically painted flowers and shrubs – such as the strewn roses with their cut stems uppermost.

The Wilton Diptych can be compared superficially to some contemporary panel paintings and manuscript illuminations, but fundamentally to none. Its sources are eclectic and the origins of its painter have been hotly debated. It has been called Italian,[1] Bohemian,[2] French[3] and English.[4] A comparison of its iconography, style and technique with contemporary works may perhaps lead to some general conclusions regarding the artist and his origins.

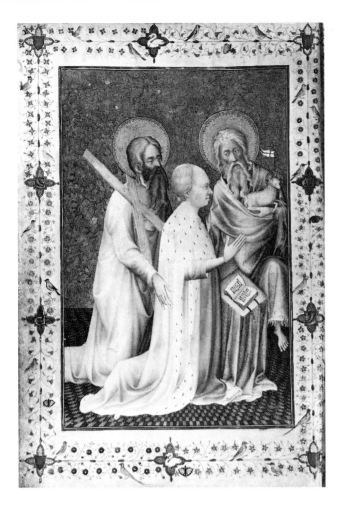

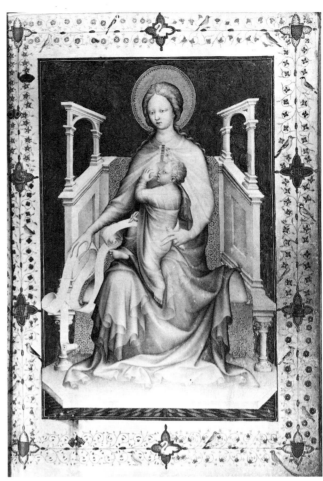

Echoes of Italy

The right-hand panel has been characterised by some
writers as Parisian and the left-hand panel as Sienese,[5]
and indeed the tousle-headed Saint John the Baptist
with his yellowish-white knotted waist band is commonly found in Sienese painting of the early fourteenth century. The motif of two onlookers, one
with an arm around the other's shoulders, the other
with folded arms, found in the two angels immediately to the right of the Virgin, first occurs in the fres-
coes by Giotto in the Peruzzi Chapel in Santa Croce,
Florence, and was widely disseminated. But most significantly perhaps, this motif and that of the angels
with folded arms are to be found in the works of the
Sienese painter Simone Martini, whose refinement of
technique finds a rare match in the Wilton Diptych.

It seems certain that the painter of the Wilton
Diptych had seen works by Simone – not necessarily
in Italy – and reflected his admiration in his own style.
Some of Simone's paintings were in Avignon, where
he died in 1344, and contact with works of art there
would have been comparatively easy. Also, the small
scale of Simone's paintings made them eminently
portable. For example, some were said to be in Dijon,
and links between the English and the Burgundian
courts were close.

The French Connection

The close ties between the English and French courts
have led several writers to explore the connections
between the Wilton Diptych and French painting of
the end of the fourteenth century. There is no exist-
ing panel painting with which it can be directly compared, but one has to take into account the discrep-
ancy between the large number of documented
paintings made for the French court and the handful
of works which survive.[6]

The small scale of the diptych and the refinement
of execution inevitably invite comparison with manuscript illumination, and the diptych has undeniable
stylistic and iconographic links with the work of the
French painters and illuminators André Beauneveu
and Jacquemart de Hesdin;[7] for example, the Virgin's
face and the unusual way in which she holds the
Child's foot resemble the Virgin's face and pose in the
Pierpont Morgan Library Sketchbook (Fig. 23).[8]

The most direct comparison with French manuscripts which can be made is with a miniature in the
Book of Hours now in Brussels (Fig. 22), which was
painted before 1402, possibly around 1390.[9] It shows the
donor, Jean, Duc de Berry (1340–1414), being presented to the Virgin and Child enthroned by Saints
Andrew and John the Baptist, with the Berry swans

ornamenting the margins. A distinction is made between the left-hand page with its drôleries, and the right-hand page with its music-making angels in the background, similar to the distinction made in the Wilton Diptych between the different patterns punched in the gold background in the left and right-hand panels, and between the wasteland and heavenly meadow.

Richard's library contained a number of French books of poetry and romance,[10] and friendship between the French and English courts led to exchanges of books among other gifts. In 1389 Philip the Bold of Burgundy gave Richard some illuminated manuscripts, and at the marriage of Richard and Isabelle, Richard received as a present the Belleville Breviary painted by Jean Pucelle around 1325.[11] According to the French chronicler Froissart, there were works by André Beauneveu in England[12] and Froissart presented an illuminated copy of one of his own works to Richard II in 1398.

Bohemian Sculpture

The mobility of objects is also relevant to a discussion of the origin of the pose of the Virgin and Child in the Wilton Diptych. It has been suggested above that there are links with French manuscripts, but the source of the pose may well be found in Bohemia.

The possibility of Bohemian influence was first suggested in the nineteenth century, but has since found little support.[13] However, the distinctive stance of the Virgin and Child cannot be found in English or French manuscript painting or sculpture, but may derive from some of the most famous images in Bohemia, where a large number of paintings and sculptures of the Virgin and Child survive from the fourteenth century.[14] The standing Virgin with her head slightly bent to look at the Child, the diagonally presented Child, counterbalancing the S-swing of her pose and leaning outward (Plate 24), derives from the type of 'Schöne Madonna' common in Bohemia,[15] of which the statue known as the Krumlov Madonna (Plate 23),[16] now in Vienna, is one of the outstanding prototypes. It is closely related to the Wilton Diptych, particularly in the position of the Child's legs (the arms of the Child in the Vienna statue are largely missing but he could have been blessing). There exist a number of derivations, including that in Prague (Fig. 24),[17] and several variants.[18] Some of the Madonnas are made of stone, and some of limewood, and they range in height from 84 cm to 116.5 cm. Only one example is dated – a statue documented as having been made in 1393.[19] The Krumlov Madonna was probably made some time before 1400, possibly

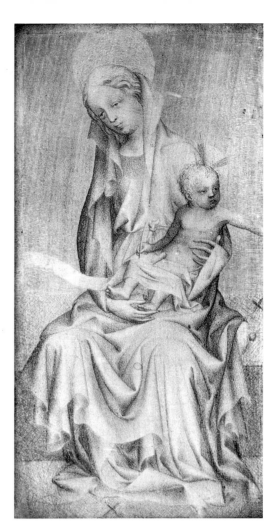

Fig. 23 *The Virgin and Child.* Circle of Jacquemart de Hesdin, c.1400. Metalpoint on boxwood, washed with white. New York, Pierpont Morgan Library, MS 346, f.1 v.

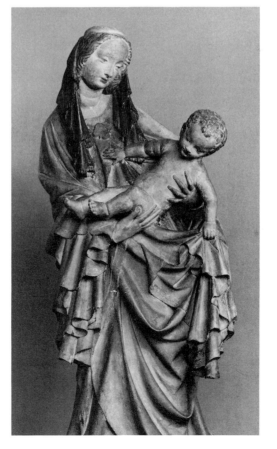

Fig. 24 Statue of the Virgin and Child (version of the Krumlov Madonna). Bohemian, c.1390–1400. Stone, 116.5 cm high. Prague, Národní Galerie.

as early as 1392.[20] It is just possible that the painter of the diptych had seen the statue in Prague. It is more likely, however, that before she died in June 1394 Queen Anne was given a similar statue, possibly a version in which the Virgin is holding the Child's foot – as in a later sculpture now in Cracow (Muzeum Narodowe)[21] – and that this was used as a model by the painter of the diptych. This particular iconography was apparently not repeated in England, even in the contemporary and later manuscripts which have been said to bear some relationship to the diptych (see for example Plate 29). This would seem to suggest that the image was not widely available in England. As we have seen, the imagery of the diptych was intensely personal to Richard and the painting would have had even more significance for him if he had felt that he was in essence kneeling before a statue of the Virgin which had belonged to his now dead and much-mourned wife.

English Sources

The sources of the iconography so far discussed have been Italian, French and Bohemian. One feature may be English, and that is the animal head still attached to John the Baptist's camel skin. This is not found in contemporary Italian, French or Bohemian painting. Although it occurs in later Flemish manuscripts, of specific interest is that it is found in English stained glass, such as in the mid-fourteenth-century north window of St Denys Walmgate, York, and most notably in the window of Winchester College where Richard kneels before John the Baptist (see Plate 16). It is also found in English pilgrim badges (Fig. 25).[22] In all these examples the head hangs down between the Baptist's legs; in the Wilton Diptych the painter has neatly moved it to the side.

An English Artist?

Since it is very likely that the Wilton Diptych was personally commissioned by Richard himself, it is logical to begin with the assumption that it was painted by an artist working at the English court.

From at least the second half of the thirteenth century there was a tradition of court patronage at Westminster. The painters working for Henry III were of international extraction,[23] and included William of Florence, John of St Omer and Peter of Hispaniae, as well as English artists. Working for Edward III from 1351 onwards was Master Hugh of St Albans; one of the members of his workshop was probably Gilbert Prince. With Master Hugh began a succession of

court painters – Gilbert Prince, Thomas Prince alias Lytlington, Thomas Wright and Thomas Kent – which lasted until 1424.[24]

A number of writers have attributed the diptych to either Gilbert Prince[25] or Thomas Lytlington,[26] the two court painters contemporary with the likely date of the diptych. Gilbert Prince had become the king's painter by 1377 and died in 1396.[27] Thomas Lytlington, who succeeded him, accompanied the king to Ireland in 1399, and is last recorded in 1401.[28]

The first problem in attributing the diptych to either of these two painters is that only a very few panel paintings, wall paintings, or manuscript illuminations survive which are definitely connected with Richard's court. They include the damaged and much-restored tester from the tomb of the Black Prince (died 1376) in Canterbury Cathedral,[29] the badly damaged tester for the joint tomb of Anne and Richard in Westminster Abbey,[30] the heavily restored portrait of Richard enthroned (Plate 26), the fairly crude paintings of the white hart in the chapel of St Mary de la Pew and on the wall of the muniment room in Westminster Abbey (see Fig. 9), and the badly damaged wall paintings in the Byward Tower in the Tower of London, as well as a few manuscripts known to have been made for Richard in which the quality of illumination is somewhat mediocre.[31] There is nothing which can be attributed to a named artist. The dangers of attributing paintings which happen to survive to painters who happen to be recorded are evident.

The second main problem is that there are no known contracts, payments or items in inventories which record any panel paintings being commissioned by Richard, let alone from either of the two recorded court painters. Most of the works mentioned are for the heraldic ephemera connected with festivals, entertainments and ceremonial occasions such as tournaments, birthdays and funerals at the court. Gilbert Prince was commissioned to paint banners for funerals, jousts and for minstrels' trumpets, to paint the royal barge and to produce designs for robes.

Thomas Lytlington is similarly documented as painting heraldic objects: banners, shields, pennons. No painters other than these two are mentioned in the surviving records of commissions for the king. It has been suggested that a large payment of just over £700 made to Thomas Lytlington in 1396–8 for various works, banners, painting and pensions could include payment for the Wilton Diptych.[32] However, there is no evidence for this apart from the possible coincidence of date and the fact that the diptych was presumably an expensive object.

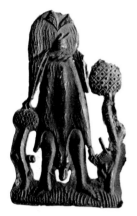

Fig. 25 Saint John the Baptist (missing the head). Pilgrim Badge, 14th century. Pewter, 4.5 cm high. Museum of London.

As has been said, the small scale and refinement of technique of the diptych invite comparison with manuscript illumination. A complicating factor is that the history of manuscript illumination in England at the end of the fourteenth and the beginning of the fifteenth century is difficult to chart because of the lack of dated works and documented artists; furthermore, several hands frequently contributed to a single volume.[33] A number of different workshops were painting in different styles, producing luxury manuscripts such as the Lytlington Missal made for the Abbot of Westminster Abbey in 1383,[34] the Lapworth Missal dated 1398, probably painted by a Netherlandish artist,[35] and the *Liber Regalis* (Plate 25), possibly painted by a Bohemian artist, around 1390–9 (see p.61). The most convincing stylistic parallels which have been drawn are with manuscripts produced in England in the early fifteenth century.

The naturalism found in the diptych[36] has for instance some parallel with the work of the English miniaturist and Dominican friar John Siferwas and his workshop, including the large Missal (Plate 29) painted for the Benedictine Abbey in Sherborne between 1395 and 1407, and the Gospel Lectionary commissioned as a gift for Salisbury Cathedral by John, Lord Lovell of Tichmarsh (died 1408).[37] However, the closest comparison between the style of the diptych and manuscript illumination is to be found in the works of the foreign illuminator Herman Scheerre and his workshop, active in England at the beginning of the fifteenth century. One scholar wrote that 'the Wilton Diptych may be said to transplant the style of Herman Scheerre and his associates to the exacting medium of panel painting'.[38] Scheerre's only definitely signed work is a Book of Offices and Prayers (London, British Library, Additional MS 16998) which has not only the signature but also the motto 'Omnia levia sunt amanti' (To the lover all things are light), which recurs in three other manuscripts associated with him.[39] Of these manuscripts the Beaufort Book of Hours (see Plate 30) and the Bedford Hours and Psalter (see Plates 27 and 28), which contains his name in the inscriptions 'I am herman your servant' and 'herman your meke servant', were considered by one scholar to be 'the only two works which stylistically can be related to the Wilton Diptych'.[40]

The signed manuscript (Additional MS 16998) contains inscriptions in Low German, which have led to Scheerre being identified with a Herman of Cologne mentioned in London in two wills of 1407.[41] The difficulty is that the Wilton Diptych does not resemble the surviving manuscripts closely enough to be attributed to the same hand as any of them. Moreover, if one accepts that the diptych was painted during Richard's lifetime, it cannot have been made after 1399, whereas the only definitely datable work associated with Herman Scheerre and his workshop falls somewhat later – namely the Bedford Hours and Psalter – a manuscript made for John of Lancaster, created duke in 1414.[42] Some writers[43] have argued that Herman Scheerre may have been working at Richard's court, having arrived there following the alliance between Richard and the Duke of Guelder in 1389, the same year as a Herman of Cologne is documented as working for the Duke.

There are other documented artists working for members of the court whose work does not survive. A certain John Prince (possibly a son of Gilbert) painted curlews, doves and popinjays in silver and gold and other colours for a banquet which Henry of Derby gave for Richard in 1397.[44] Richard's Chancellor, William of Wykeham, who commissioned the window showing the king in Winchester (Plate 16), employed a certain Herebright, painter of London, whose equipment was carried from Esher to Farnham in April 1393: he is probably identifiable with the Herebright of Cologne who painted an altarpiece for St Paul's Cathedral in 1398.[45]

The Technique of the Wilton Diptych

The Wilton Diptych – despite its primarily religious function – was also a luxury object whose jewel-like appearance would have been intended for close scrutiny. This is apparent from the elaborate optical effects set up by contrasting methods of treating the gold; from the surface enriched with thickly applied paint and with translucent coloured glazes; and from the fine detail of the painted surface. Some of this richness has now been lost: some of the glazes have worn away, some of the pigments have faded, and some areas have suffered damage, notably the cap of maintenance and part of the foliage around the hart on the exterior, and Richard's hands and two of the angels' faces on the interior.

Although meticulous care went into its execution, a few significant changes were made not only at the stage between the preliminary drawing and the actual painting – as one might expect – but even once the final painting had been begun. Moreover, some areas were not completed, and it is impossible to say whether they were deliberately abandoned or left unfinished for a reason beyond the painter's control.

Analysis of the technical features makes it clear that it was executed by a single workshop, but the origins of that workshop are elusively obscure. The diptych was cleaned in 1992 (see pp.86–7) and during this time a technical investigation was undertaken to try to determine whether the method of its execution could in any way clarify the origins of the painter.[46]

The Structure of the Diptych

The diptych is painted on both sides of two panels identified as oak, a wood commonly used by North European panel painters. Each panel measures approximately 47.5 by 29.2 cm. The panel with the Virgin and Child is a single plank of wood, whereas the panel with Richard and the saints consists of two pieces joined vertically. The frame on both is carved out of the same piece of wood as the painted panels.

This apparently simple structure has some puzzling features. X-radiographs (Fig. 26) show that in the Virgin/heraldic panel there are two interruptions of the oak grain at the top left and bottom left-hand corners, each measuring approximately 3.8 × 8 cm, and each apparently revealing a much finer grain than the

rest of the oak, which is regular, straight and vertical. It is virtually inconceivable that the panels chosen would have had faults which needed patching or repair. These patches, which are symmetrical and placed in identical positions top and bottom, are at present inexplicable. They may represent paper or parchment rectangles attached to the wood beneath the ground, but they are inaccessible to examination.

The wings are joined by two hinges made of iron, which are original and have traces of a layer of gilding, which would have made them less obtrusive. X-radiographs show that level with the two hinges are four rectangular tapered metal insertions, subsequently concealed at the edges by the chalk ground. These are identical in size and shape to the flanges of the hinges, which are embedded in the frame. There could be two explanations for these insertions. More panels may have been planned on either side – although a work of more than two rectangular panels would have been cumbersome and difficult to close; moreover, the compositional coherence shows that the diptych is a complete object. A more likely possibility is that clasps were originally intended, but it was decided at an early stage, before the chalk ground was applied, not to use them, since the chalk ground covers the sides continuously. There is no evidence of clasps having been applied to the exterior, and it seems likely that the diptych would have had a pouch of either leather or cloth which kept the panels together when closed.[47]

From the damaged area on the Virgin/heraldic panel it is possible to see that the oak panels were covered first with a mat of 'fibres',[48] which, unusually, seem to be derived from parchment, apparently applied directly onto the wood,[49] and then with a layer of natural chalk (Fig. 27),[50] commonly used by North European painters as the ground for painting. No fibre was laid on the frames, where a moderately thick layer of chalk was directly applied. The fibres seem intended to reinforce the adhesion of the ground to the panel, in a manner similar to the woven fabrics applied to strengthen the gesso in Italian panel paintings of this period. Cracks in the ground which are continuous from the main panel to the edges of the frame show that the covering with chalk ground was done in a single phase of execution.

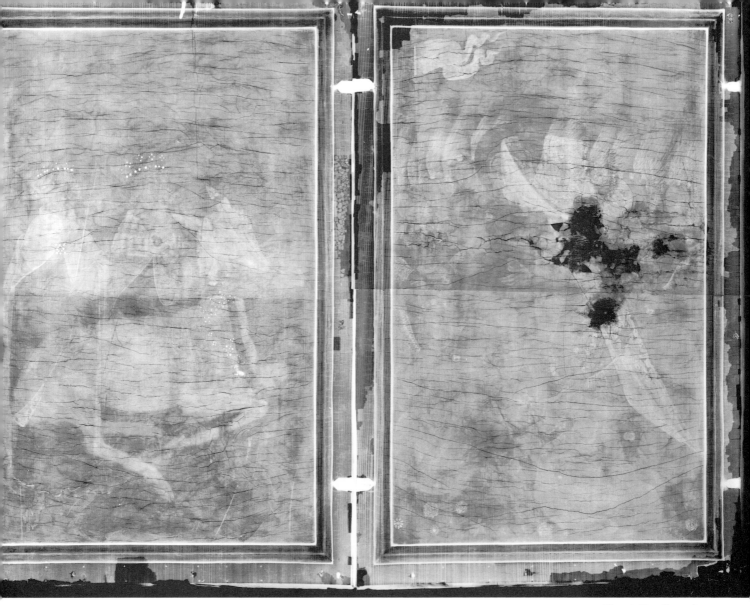

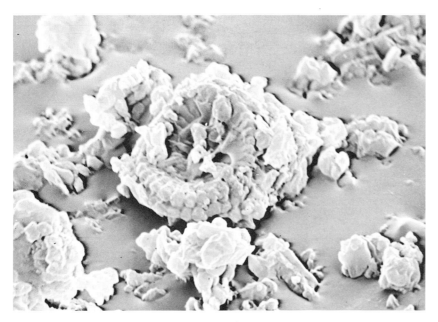

Fig. 26 X-radiograph of the Wilton Diptych. The metal of the original iron hinges embedded in the frame shows as solid white, and the lead white of the painted pearls in the Richard/hart panel (left) is equally dense. In the Virgin/heraldic panel (right) the irregular black patches near the centre of the image are the damages in the heraldic panel.

Fig. 27 Scanning electron microscope micrograph of a sample of ground showing a microfossil coccolith, indicating that the chalk ground is of natural origin. Magnification 5,320×.

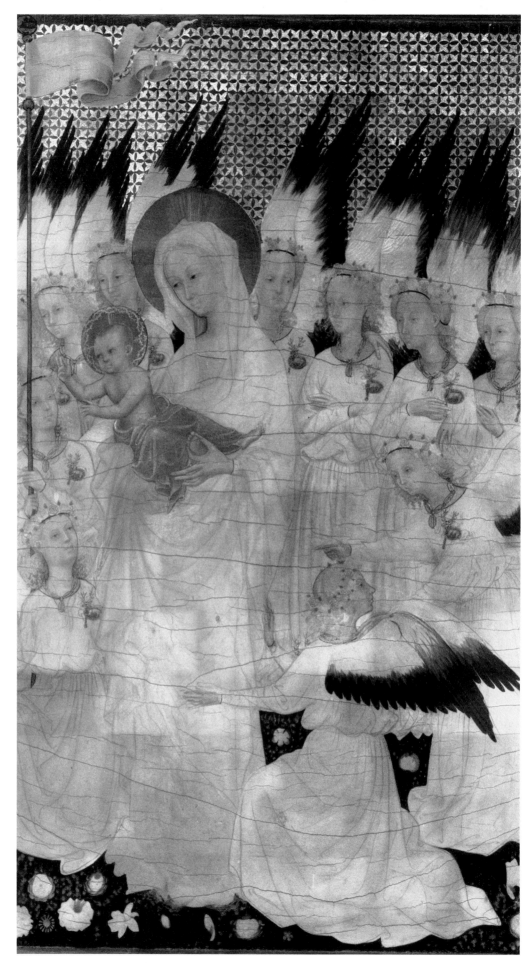

Fig. 28 Infra-red
reflectogram mosaic,
assembled by
computer, of the panel
with the Virgin and
Child showing the
underdrawing, which
is most visible in the
draperies and hands.

76

The Design of the Composition

The composition was first sketched in detail directly onto the white ground. This drawing is revealed by infra-red photography (Fig. 28). It is difficult to be certain whether it was done with metalpoint or with some form of ink. Possibly both were used.[51] Examination of the underdrawing visible beneath the drapery folds of Saint Edward's robe seems under high magnification to indicate at least a partial use of the brush: the feathery split lines resemble those outlining the shaft of Saint Edmund's arrow, which was certainly painted with a brush. The drawing was followed precisely in the painting with the exception of a very few small *pentimenti*. For example, there are small changes in the hands of two of the angels: significantly, the position of the pointing finger of the standing angel at the right-hand side (Fig. 29) was lowered to point more directly at Richard, focusing the composition more emphatically on him; also the hands of the angel kneeling at the bottom right-hand corner were made slightly smaller. There was a reduction in scale of all the broomcod collars and harts of the angels (Fig. 30). Some details such as the feathering of the angels' wings were not drawn, but delineated only in the final painting.

The painter adapted his technique according to the scale of the image. The larger scale of the images on the exterior has led to some differences in the underdrawing, which might more accurately be called undermodelling. The infra-red reflectograms show that the red cap of maintenance and the hart were first outlined, probably with a brush. Broad washes of undermodelling were then used to sketch in the cap and hart, establishing their form and defining light and shade. This is particularly clear in the hart (Fig. 31). Wide brushstrokes define the contour and tonality of the anatomy, for example on the chest and forequarters, and the modelling is graduated to give a three-dimensional effect.

The Gilding of the Panels and Tooling of the Gold

After the major elements of the composition had been established by drawing, the gold backgrounds and mouldings of the frame were water gilded in a conventional manner, the gold being applied to an adhesive base of reddish-brown bole and burnished. The gold is in extremely good condition. Only on the interior is the gilding worn, where the frame was handled when the diptych was opened and closed. The helm above the shield on the exterior panel was originally silver leaf, modelled with stippling: the

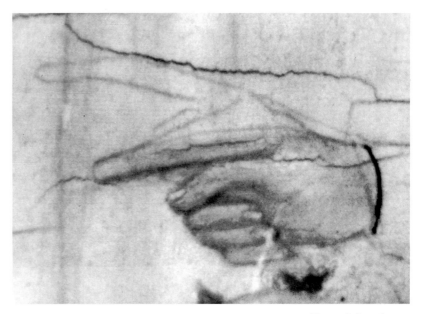

Fig. 29 Infra-red reflectogram showing the underdrawing of the pointing angel's right hand, particularly the change to the index finger.

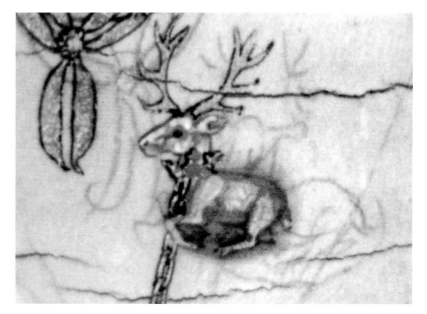

Fig. 30 Infra-red reflectogram showing the underdrawing of an angel's broomcod collar and white hart badge, and the changes in position and reduction in scale made in the final image.

silver has now tarnished and blackened and only vestiges remain (see Plates 4 and 5).

After the gold and silver leaf had been applied, the outlines of the figures to be painted were incised to give a clear definition of the limits of the paint. These limits have been followed very precisely and can now be seen where the paint abuts the gold of the background. The lack of flaking along the edges indicates that very little paint overlaps the gold, for in those areas where paint has been applied over gold, the paint has flaked very considerably, as in the fur lining of the sleeves of Edmund's and Richard's robes.

An early change of plan is evident in the left wing where the presence of bole under the forest shows that this area was intended to be gilded. It may be that the space between John the Baptist and the frame was thought to be too stark and the division between the two groups too marked when gilded, and so the space was filled with the forest.

One of the distinctive features of the diptych is the variety of ways in which stippling using a single dot punch has been used, both for patterning and for modelling, creating subtle effects which exploit the optical qualities of the changing fall of light. The punching was probably done by exerting pressure with a small metal tool, rather than by tapping the punch with a mallet, because of the delicate, light and precise touch needed to indent the gold but not break its surface.

The gold background of each interior panel has a faintly incised square grid which formed a guide for the pattern carried out in the fine dot punch. A floral pattern was created in the left wing (Plates 31 and 32) and a foliate pattern in the right wing to act as a foil for the painted areas and to contrast with the plain burnished gold in the haloes of the three saints in the left panel. Apart from the three plain haloes, the rays incised in the Virgin's halo, and those parts executed in mordant gilding (see below), almost every available surface of the gold has been densely tooled with the fine stipple. In the case of the Child's halo it has been used to create a crown of thorns and three nails (see Plate 20), which replace the usual cross. The crowns of Edmund and Edward have been stippled in order to make them stand out against the plain surface of their untooled haloes (see Plates 15 and 33). This sort of stippling also decorated actual jewellery, such as the crown supposed to have belonged to Anne of Bohemia (Fig. 1). Elsewhere the stippling in the birds of Edmund's robe (Plate 37) and brooch, in the harts and broomcods of Richard's robe (Plate 38), in his sleeve and the fringe of his collar, and in the ring held by Edward (Plate 41), catches the light with shimmering effect.

The most astonishing display of virtuosity is in the handling of the punch where it is used for modelling. This is particularly outstanding in the folds of the Child's robe (Plate 35): here the punch has been used most densely where the folds project, as on the Child's knee, and the gold left untooled in the recessive folds. On the exterior heraldic panel punching has been used to create the details of the muzzle and eyes of the lion's face (Plate 34). The antlers of the white hart on the exterior have been entirely modelled with stippling (Plate 36), without recourse to any painted outline but relying totally on the fall of light to make them stand out against the plain burnished background. The stippling has been done in clusters, becoming denser from one edge to the other and denser in the tips.

As well as water gilding, some details were applied in mordant gilding to give a raised effect to small details such as the angels' broomcod collars,[52] the antlers of the angels' harts and the harts' chains pendant from the crowns, with rectangular links and a final circular ring (Plate 14). To work such tiny details in mordant gilding required great skill and precision.

In some cases the gold has been outlined with a fine painted black line. On the interior panels Richard's crown and broomcod collar and the antlers of his hart jewel, the Child's halo, part of the Virgin's halo, and the angels' broomcod collars were all outlined in black to give them greater prominence. On the exterior, as elsewhere in the diptych, some features were begun and not completed: the crown around the hart's neck has been punched and one florette only partly outlined in black, and the first two links of the chain have been punched but not the rest.

One of the optical contrasts set up by the painter is that between burnished and unburnished gold. While most of the gold is burnished, the fleurs-de-lis on the right-hand side of the shield on the exterior panel (see Plate 5) have been applied with mordant gilding and then have been left unburnished, their matt appearance contrasting with the gold cross and birds on the left-hand side. Here the burnished gold background is simply left exposed, with the blue apparently painted around the forms rather than painted over the whole and then scraped away – as found in the gold fabrics of the robes.

The technique of the gold fabrics follows the *sgraffito* method, practised for example by fourteenth-century Italian panel painters.[53] Here it is on a particularly finely detailed scale. Richard's robe (Plate 38) was gilded, then thinly painted with vermilion which was then scraped away to expose the gold design of broomcods encircling harts lodged among

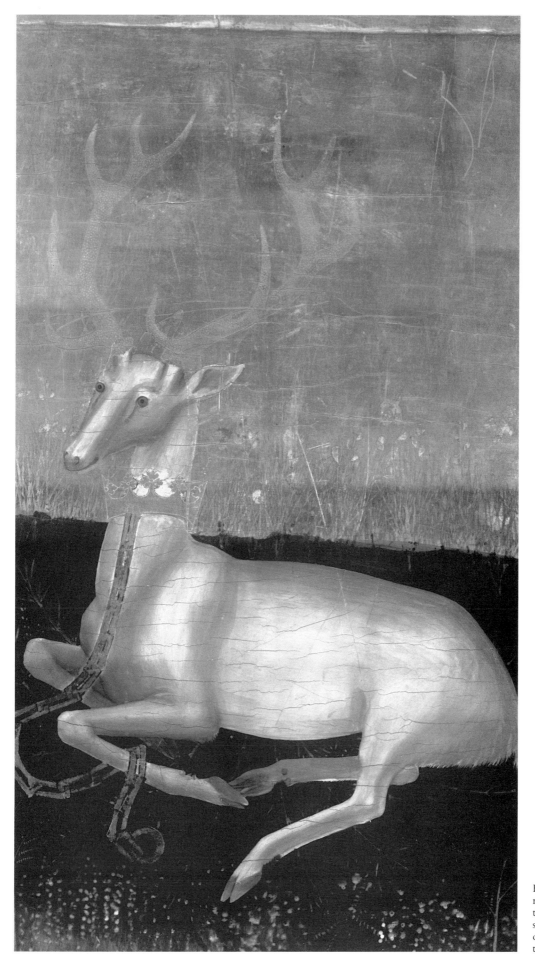

Fig. 31 Infra-red
reflectogram mosaic of
the white hart panel
showing the modelling
of the body beneath
the final paint layer.

rosemary. In the next stage the gold ground was densely stippled. Finally the glazes (see below) were added to pick out the folds. Examination has shown that the vermilion paint on Richard's robe has darkened a fraction at its surface; the original effect would have been even more striking than it is today.[54]

The same *sgraffito* method was used for the design of Edmund's robe (Plate 37) with lapis lazuli ultramarine, although in this case it appears from the identical repetition of the image that a cartoon was used for the pattern of cranes or phoenixes linked by crowns, with spurs or suns pendant from the crowns. Unlike in Richard's robe, the blue was strengthened around the pattern and then straight vertical folds applied, with a saturated brush going straight over the pattern. In one place where the design left an unpatterned patch, a foliate design was inserted to fill the gap. A small pink and white tassle or cloud was painted below each spur or sun. Just below Edmund's brooch a minute streak of white with small red jewel-like dots of glaze, only visible under high magnification, indicates a change of plan in the robe, although what was originally intended is difficult to determine. The area below the right shoulder and across the remains of the belt has been damaged, exposing the orange of the bole.

The Painting

Whereas the support (oak) and the ground (chalk) are characteristic of North European panel painting, the painting technique and some of the pigments are characteristic of Italian painters. The medium of all the painted areas, with the exception of the blue of the shield,[55] has been identified as egg.[56] The optical effects of this are quite specific:[57] it enables the painter to exploit the full purity of colour of certain pigments, particularly that of ultramarine, as demonstrated outstandingly in the Virgin panel, where all the draperies are painted in this pigment.

As also in paintings from fourteenth-century Italy, where the technique of egg tempera painting was widely practised, the undermodelling of the faces, hands and feet has been done in a pale bluish green identified as *terra verde* (green earth),[58] mixed with lead white (Plate 39). This undermodelling can be clearly seen in some damaged areas, such as the face of the angel immediately to the right of the Virgin. The flesh tones have been built up with a series of hatched strokes as required by the egg tempera technique, in this case the brushstrokes are of exceptional fineness and delicacy.

The original appearance of the diptych has also been affected by changes undergone by some of the pigments, notably the reds. For instance, several of the red lake pigments have faded. This particularly applies to Saint Edward's robe where lines of a brownish-red glaze survive in the shadows and folds, in both outer and inner garments (Plate 44). These now appear mainly white, but must originally have been a warmer pinkish colour which has entirely faded and is difficult to reconstruct in the mind's eye. The pink roses in the angels' chaplets would originally have been more scarlet, emphasising the contrast between alternating red and white flowers.

Certain of the pigment mixtures used in the diptych are extremely complex but are consistent from one panel to another, confirming that the diptych was executed in a single phase. For example, cross-sections of paint samples (Plates 45–48) show that the foliage on which the white hart on the exterior lies was painted in exactly the same way as the foliage in the scene with the Virgin and Child with angels on the interior, and the inference is that a single workshop, probably a single artist, was responsible throughout.[59] The leaves of the rosemary branches on which the hart is lying were painted with a mixed green containing greenish azurite, lead white and possibly some yellow lake or other form of dyestuff-based pigment, a mixture found also in the deep green robe of Saint Edmund on the interior panel. Similarly, the greyish white of the cap of maintenance has been painted in an identical layer structure to the white of the hart.

A number of distinct and complex techniques were used for the greens in the foliage in the hart panel in order to differentiate between the various plants. The greens of the two small branching ferns at either corner of the foreground have been made like the rosemary with mixtures of blue and yellow but using different pigments, this time azurite combined with a particular form of the artificial pigment lead tin yellow[60] and possibly also yellow lake. Yet another mixed green was found in the small round-leafed plants. This was made with natural orpiment combined with indigo.[61] The stems of the irises were painted in a quite different technique, with a thin translucent layer of deep blue-green indigo. The effect is that of a green glaze, enhanced by the gilding underneath where the stems reach above the horizon. The yellow glaze of the iris petals has mostly flaked or faded, leaving only a silhouette of the flowers against the gold leaf.

The painted surface was originally extremely rich. Unfortunately some of the jewel-like effects of glazes are no longer as striking as they once were: the crowns had jewels of different colours, some of which are now missing or have darkened (see Plates 15 and

33), and in each of the angels' collars one of the two pendant pods has a green glaze, now visible only under a microscope. Other glazes which are diminished in their effect are in Richard's robe, which was not originally as flat as it now appears: glazed lines of red and yellow-green lake suggesting folds fan out from the wrist, and are painted over the fringes and the collar and sleeve. These are just visible with oblique illumination and by viewing the panel at an angle. The remnants of a deep red glaze can still be detected on the part of his robe covering his breast.

The surface of the painting is also remarkably three-dimensional. Apart from the mordant gilding already discussed, a thickly applied lead white is skilfully used to create a raised effect. The harts of the badges are painted with a thick lead white enabling the painter to detail the anatomy against a green background, the white being then finely outlined in brown (Plate 14). Raised lead white is also used to achieve the illusion of pearls decorating the crowns (Plate 33), Edmund's brooch (Plate 40), Richard's broomcod collar, and the antlers of Richard's hart jewel (Plate 8). The buttons on Edward's blue sleeve are also raised but this appears to have been achieved with blobs of chalk, in the manner of *pastiglia* (Plate 41).

The painter has exploited the precision and fineness possible with egg tempera in order to detail highlights on faces, fingertips, eyelashes, and locks of hair, fluffy feathers of wings etc. The colours of the figures' eyes are consciously varied despite the fact that the differences are not immediately obvious on such a small scale: some of the figures have blue, some grey, some brown eyes.

In contrast to the meticulous planning which went into the first laying out of the design, and the careful attention to detail, there are a number of minute changes of plan in the final painted layer. For example, the chaplet of the uppermost angel at the extreme left originally had a more continuous band of greenery, which was reduced to single leaves for the rest of the angels, except that to the immediate right of the Virgin where the intervening leaves between the roses of the chaplet are in trefoils. The wings of the angel kneeling in the right-hand corner have a thin layer of pale pink underpaint and fine green bars on the feathers of the right wing not found on any of the other angels' wings (Plate 43). Uniquely, the feathers of the wings of the angel immediately to the right of the Virgin have been picked out with thin lines of red paint (Plate 42).

Conclusion

The consistency of technique found in all four scenes of the Wilton Diptych suggests that it was painted in a single phase of execution. The continuity of the chalk ground and gilding from interior to exterior, the identical pigment mixtures to be found on both interior and exterior panels, and the unity of style in both the punching and the painting all make it likely that only one artist was involved. Nevertheless, close-knit collaboration can never be entirely ruled out, particularly given that the coat of arms is in a different medium and seems less skilful than the rest of the painting. The artist concerned was a highly accomplished draughtsman and craftsman, adept in employing a variety of techniques to achieve a range of decorative and optical effects. He contrasts matt unburnished gold with shining burnished gold, plain shining gold with densely stippled textured gold, and flat gold with the raised effects of mordant gilding and thickly applied lead white. Laid over the gold are many rich glazes to simulate jewels or enrich the modelling of drapery. Highly complicated mixtures of pigment are used, but also unadulterated ultramarine dominates with breathtaking simplicity in the right-hand panel, where all the figures except the Child are in blue and yet each figure has its own spatial coherence.

The techniques are a combination of northern and Italian methods. The oak support and chalk ground were commonly used by northern painters, while egg tempera and undermodelling of flesh painting with green earth are typical of Italian technique and suggest a direct familiarity with Italian practice. However, the scarcity of surviving works, of which only a few have been analysed,[62] make it difficult to set these techniques in context. They seem not to conform to English practice, where oil was more commonly used. In reality the international nature of the European courts encouraged artists to travel from one court to another, learning new techniques and exchanging pigments and materials. The extremely personal nature of the heraldic emblems and themes of the diptych suggest that the artist was working at the court of Richard II in close collaboration with the king, while the eclectic sources of the iconography and technique suggest that he was well-travelled. Perhaps one should best describe this artist as neither Italian, French, Bohemian nor English but truly European.

What Became of the Wilton Diptych?

In August 1399, on his way back from Ireland, Richard II was captured by the troops of his cousin, Henry of Derby, son of John of Gaunt.[63] On 1 September he was taken to London, to Westminster and then to the Tower, and on 29 September he resigned the crown to Henry IV (Fig. 32). He was taken to various castles and eventually imprisoned at Pontefract, one of Henry's castles in the heartland of the Lancastrian estate, which was destroyed by Cromwell's troops during the Civil War. There he was murdered, probably starved to death. On 17 February 1400 his body was taken to London where it was put on display, covered with lead and with only the head exposed. Richard was then buried in King's Langley, and it was not until 1413 in the reign of Henry V, that his body was transferred to the tomb he had commissioned for himself in Westminster Abbey.

Where the Wilton Diptych was when Richard was captured is unknown. He may have taken it with him to Ireland. If so, it may be relevant that some of the king's jewels, goods and chattels and the goods of the magnates of the realm who were with him on his last voyage to Ireland went astray and the king's serjeant at arms was ordered to seek to recover them in the port of Bristol or in Cornwall or Devon, or wherever they could be found.[64]

The earliest record of the diptych is in the collection of Charles I, who was said to have acquired it from a certain Lady Jennings in return for a portrait of the king by the Dutch painter Jan Lievens.[65] While it was in the king's collection it was engraved by Hollar in 1639.

The diptych is next recorded in the collection of the Earls of Pembroke at Wilton House from which it takes its name. It was said to have been given by King James II to Lord Castlemain when he went as ambassador to Rome, and bought from his heirs after his death in 1705 by Thomas Earl of Pembroke.[66]

It remained at Wilton House until 1929 when it entered the Collection of the National Gallery. Its acquisition brought it to public attention and prompted a number of scholarly studies which bear witness to its continuing power to puzzle and to enchant.

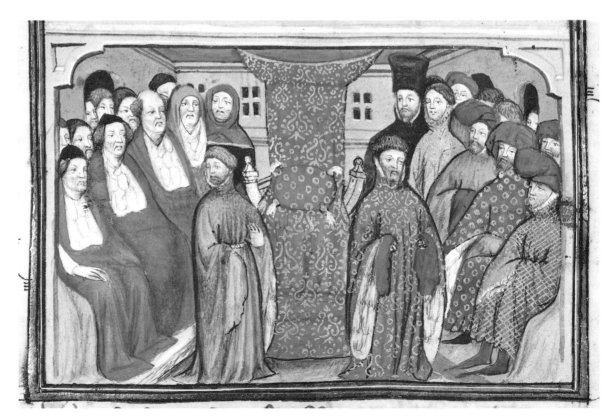

Fig. 32 *Henry Bolingbroke claims the empty throne after Richard II's deposition.* French, mid-15th century. London, British Library, Harley MS 1319, f.57.

NOTES

1. Waagen said it was 'without doubt by a very able Italian painter, who probably lived at the court of Richard II' (Waagen 1854, III, pp.150–1); in 1857 he called it Sienese (Waagen 1857, p.2, no.42).

2. Scharf 1882, pp.72–3.

3. Borenius and Tristram 1927, pp.27–8 (close to the Berry Book of Hours and the *Epître de Philippe de Mézières*); Constable, BM, 1929, p.45 ('a painter of the French school in close contact with André Beauneveu'); Lemoisne 1931, pp.57–8 (close to the Narbonne altar frontal); Borenius, *Pantheon*, 1936, pp.209–14 (by French manuscript illuminator, close to Jacquemart de Hesdin); Sterling, 1942, pp.20 and 78–9, n.22 (Parisian *c.*1377).

4. Popham, *Apollo,* 1928, pp.317–18 (style similar to that of André Beauneveu, but probably by an English artist); Conway, BM, 1929, pp.209–12; Beard, *Connoisseur*, 1931, p.375 (by an English artist familiar with the 'idiosyncrasies of English armoury'); Cripps-Day, *Connoisseur*, 1933, pp.167–9; Shaw, BM, 1934, pp.175–81; Evans, *Archaeological Journal*, 1950, p.5.

5. Mathew 1968, p.199. Rickert (1965, p.159) saw 'discrepancies between the two sides' in the tooling of the gold, colour scheme and composition which led her to the suggestion that 'the two wings were not painted at the same time or for the same purpose; that the left panel represents one wing of a votive diptych or perhaps a tripytch'.

6. See Lemoisne 1931, pp.44ff; Sterling 1987, *passim.*

7. e.g. Popham, *Apollo*, 1928, pp.317–18; Borenius, *Pantheon*, 1936, pp.209–14.

8. Fry, BM, x, 1906–7, pp.31–8, esp. Pl. I, where it is attributed to Beauneveu; also Meiss 1967, pp.278ff, and Fig. 279, where it is attributed to Jacquemart (?).

9. Meiss 1967, pp.198ff. and Figs. 179–180. The similarities were considered to be 'coincidental, accidental and superficial' by Tristram (*The Month*, 1949, p.29).

10. Rickert, *The Library*, XIII, 1933, pp.144–7. Rickert saw this as bearing out the view that Richard was a fantastic romantic dreamer unable to come to grips with life. Green showed that these books came under the Exchequer and were not Richard's personal reading matter and that they had been inherited and not acquired by him (Green, *The Library*, XXI, 1976, pp.235–9).

11. Paris, Bibliothèque Nationale, lat.10483–4. See Alexander 1983 pp.146ff; and Sterling 1989, pp.71ff.

12. Froissart (ed. Kervyn de Lettenhoven), XIV, 1872, p.197.

13. Bohemian influence or authorship was specifically discounted by Borenius and Tristram 1927, pp.27–8; Popham, *Apollo*, 1928, pp.317–18; Constable, BM, 1929, p.43; Fry, 1972, I, p.240. Dostal 1928, p.169, discounted Bohemian authorship, but allowed for a knowledge of contemporary Bohemian art. In favour of Bohemian authorship was Noppen, BM, 1932, p.87. Wormald, JWCI, 1954, p.193, n.6

warned against overstressing the part played by foreigners brought to Richard's court by Anne of Bohemia, and recently Simpson 1984, p.186, stated categorically that 'there is no evidence either documentary or stylistic to support the view that Bohemian painting in any way influenced English painting'.

14. See Hlavackova, *Revue de l'Art,* 1985, p.60.

15. Clasen 1974, pp.57ff. and 133ff. Until the invention of this type of Virgin and Child Bohemian sculptures tended to follow the French type with the Child held high on the Virgin's hip. See, for example, the statue of 1381 for Prague Town Hall (Clasen 1974, p.122 and Fig. 287).

16. *Die Parler* 1978, vol.2, p.686.

17. Swoboda 1969, Abb.68.

18. e.g. those from Moravsky Sternberk, Vimperik Parish Church and Pilsen (Swoboda 1969, Abb.63,71,68).

19. Bachmann in Swoboda 1969, p.133.

20. It is closely related to the panel painting of the Saint Vitus Madonna, which almost certainly derives from it, rather than vice versa. Pesina attributed the Saint Vitus and Krumlov Madonnas to the same workshop (Pesina, *Jahrbuch des Kunsthistorischen Institutes der Universität Graz*, 1972–3, Band VII, pp.20ff.). The Saint Vitus Madonna was probably painted before 1396 when the donor, Bishop Johann Jenczenstein, shown kneeling in the carved wooden frame, went to Rome, where he died in 1400. The painting has been dated as early as 1392 (*Die Parler* 1978, vol.2, p.682) which would mean that the sculpture dates from a little before 1392 (in *Die Parler*, op.cit., p.686, it is dated 1390–1400), certainly before 1396. Gerhard Schmidt (Swoboda 1969, p.242) considers the sculpture came first. He warns that in the case of the Saint Vitus Madonna the frame and the picture may not necessarily belong together and that the identity of the Bishop is open to debate (p.242). For Bishop Johann Jenczenstein see *Die Parler* 1978, vol.3, p.35.

21. Inv.no.10315. See *Die Parler* 1978, vol.2, p.489.

22. Spencer 1990, p.40.

23. Lethaby, *The Walpole Society,* 1911–12, I, pp.69–72.

24. Harvey, BM, 1947, pp.30–5.

25. Tristram, *The Month*, 1949, II, p.34.

26. Harvey, BM, 1947, p.304 and id. 1948, p.65; Tudor Craig in *Age of Chivalry*, p.135. Mathew (1968, pp.47–9) attributed the diptych to two hands: the heraldic panel to Thomas Lytlington, and the white hart panel to John Siferwas.

27. Gilbert Prince is first documented working at Westminster in 1351. He was patronised by John of Gaunt, Richard's uncle, the Duke of Lancaster. He lived in the Parish of St Giles, Cripplegate, and on 24 March 1393 was exempted for life from all public services such as serving on a jury or on a coroner's inquest (CPR 1391–6, pp.170, 178, 270). He was a leading member of the guild and in 1376 and

1384–8 Common Councillorman for Cripplegate ward. He probably ran a large workshop. On 22 January 1396 he made his will from which it is evident that he was a very wealthy man, owning a large amount of property: he left his clothing to be shared among his serving craftsmen ('famulos meos operarios') as well as his household servants, but strangely enough he willed that all instruments belonging to his art should be sold. He died in February 1396 (see Devon 1837, p.207; Wylie, IV, 1898, pp.157, 161, 170; Shaw, BM, 1934, pp.171–5; Harvey, BM, 1947, p.304; Harvey 1948, pp.61–5; Tristram, *The Month*, II, 1949, pp.34–5).

28. For Thomas Lytlington see Devon 1837, p.291; Wylie, IV, 1898, pp.172, 174, 184, 221; Harvey, BM, 1947, p.304; CPR, 1366–99, London 1909, p.573.

29. See Simpson 1980, p.139; and Simpson 1984, pp.168ff.

30. *Age of Chivalry*, p.134 and Cat. 713, p.517.

31. For the numerous portraits of Richard II see Whittingham, BM, 1971, pp.12ff. For manuscripts commissioned by Richard see Sandler 1986, p.175, nos.151 and 152.

32. Harvey, *Archaeologia*, 1961, p.7, n.3.

33. Scott 1994 (in press).

34. *Age of Chivalry*, Cat. 714.

35. *Age of Chivalry*, Cat. 717.

36. Wormald (JWCI, 1954, p.196) connected the naturalism found in the diptych with Lombard manuscript painting, particularly in the work of Giovanni de Grassi (d.1398) which includes the drawing of a hart. Harvey (*Archaeologia*, 1961, p.16, n.4) points out the 'significant differences'.

37. Joint patrons of the Sherborne Missal were Richard Mitford, Bishop of Salisbury 1395–1407, and Robert Brunyng, Abbot of Sherborne 1385–1415, both frequently depicted in the Missal. John Siferwas was a Dominican friar, documented from 1380 to 1421. See Herbert 1920; and Rickert 1965, pp.163ff. Mathew 1968, p.47, attributed the white hart of the diptych to John Siferwas.

38. Panofsky, *Early Netherlandish Painting*, 1953, p.118. See also Tristram, *The Month*, II, 1949, pp.28ff.; Clarke, BM, 1931, p.283; Shaw, BM, 1934, pp.175ff.

39. The Chester Beatty Book of Hours, the Beaufort Book of Hours (British Library, Royal MS 2.A.XVIII), and a Bible (British Library, Royal MS 1.E.IX), while his name is inscribed on the Chichele Breviary (Lambeth MS 69) and the Bedford Hours (British Library, Additional MS 42131). See Rickert, BM, 1935, p.40; and Turner, *Apollo*, 1962, pp.265–70.

40. Wormald, JWCI, 1954, pp.196ff. For Royal MS 2.A.XVIII see also Rickert, BM, 1965, pp.238–46.

41. Rickert, BM, 1935, p.39. He may be identifiable with the Herman of Cologne mentioned in the accounts of the Duke of Gelder in 1388–9 and at Dijon 1401–3 where he was paid by the Duke of Burgundy for helping Jean Malouel to paint the Calvary carved by Claus Sluter for the Chartreuse

de Champmol, and he was in Paris in 1419 (Alexander and Kauffmann 1973, p.104). If these are all the same Herman he was certainly well travelled.

42. Rickert, BM, 1935, pp. 39ff.; Kuhn, *Art Bulletin*, 1940, pp.138ff.; Rickert 1965, pp.166ff.; and Turner, *Apollo*, 1962, pp.265ff. See Wright, *British Library Journal*, 1992, pp.196–7, who supports the view of the Wilton Diptych as the product of Lancastrian patronage.

43. e.g. Rickert 1952, pp.140–1, and Mathew 1968, pp.42ff.

44. PRO, DL: 28/1/9, f.18v. I owe this reference to Caroline Barron.

45. Harvey, *The Month*, 1949, pp.433ff., and Harvey, *Archaeologia*, 1971, p.150.

46. Paint samples were prepared as cross-sections in polyester resin by standard methods. Analysis of paint layers was carried out on carbon-coated samples using energy-dispersive X-ray microanalysis (EDX) in the scanning electron microscope (SEM). All analytical spectra were acquired at 25kV. X-ray diffraction was by the Debye-Scherrer powder method, using 114mm cameras. Media analyses were by gas-chromatography linked to mass-spectrometry (GC-MS) and Fourier-transform infra-red microspectrophotometry (FTIR).

47. In the inventory of the royal possessions made in 1400 is a gold and enamel plaque kept in a leather case (Palgrave 1836, III, p.316, item 16). In the French royal accounts for 1390 are payments for a pouch for a portable round panel painting from the royal chapel (Brière, GBA, 1919, p.236, n.1). In 1401–2 Peter Swan was paid for embroidering a red velvet case for a small image of Saint Veronica for Henry IV (Wylie, IV, 1898, p.220).

48. The fibres beneath the chalk ground were identified by Josephine Darrah, Senior Scientific Officer, the Victoria and Albert Museum, as collagen and are closest to reference standards of parchment.

49. Because oak is more close-grained than poplar, northern paintings which are generally painted on oak do not have the layer of woven fabric found under the gesso in the majority of Italian panel paintings.

50. Coccoliths (microfossils) were found by scanning electron microscopy in the ground, indicating that the chalk is of natural origin.

51. Examination of a minute sample of underdrawing showed very fine (sub-micron) black particles clinging to the underside of the paint film. These appear to be composed of carbon, but positive identification of the material is difficult on samples of such small scale.

52. Mordant gilding refers to the application of gold leaf to the surface of a painted passage using a layer of adhesive (the mordant) to accept the gold. Mordants were commonly based on drying oils such as linseed, or may have been proteinaceous, such as egg, often combined with pigment to give bulk. The mordant used on the heraldic panel of

the diptych was identified as egg mixed with white and yellow-brown pigments. Decoration of a surface with mordant gilding usually produced a distinctly raised effect. The technique is quite separate from leaf gilding on to bole (water gilding), as in the background gilding of the diptych. For a fuller description of mordant gilding, see Bomford 1989, pp.43–7.

53. An account of the technique for *sgraffito* drapery designs is given in Bomford 1989, pp.130–6 and plates 115–18.

54. Vermilion is known to darken, particularly in egg tempera paint films. In Richard II's *sgraffito* robe, the change is slight and is present only in an exceedingly thin layer at the surface. However, the product of darkened vermilion pigment (black metacinnabar) is of such high refractive index and dark colour that even a slight change in the original pigment influences the tone of the paint film considerably. Here the reddish-brown colour of the paint suggests the use of an earth pigment; analysis, however, showed only vermilion to have been employed. See also R.J. Gettens, R.L. Feller and W.T. Chase, 'Vermilion and Cinnabar', in *Artists' Pigments: A Handbook of their History and Characteristics*, vol. II, edited and revised by A. Roy, National Gallery of Art, Washington D.C., in press, 1993.

55. The binding medium for the ultramarine of the shield was shown to be animal glue. Since the medium here differs from the remainder of the diptych which is painted in egg tempera (see note 56 below), perhaps a specialist heraldic painter was employed for this part, or an attempt was being made to achieve a different and distinctive optical effect in the heraldry.

56. Egg tempera was identified by R. White in samples as follows (Richard II panel): green of Saint Edmund's cloak; (Virgin and Child panel): white edge of angel's wing, left-hand side; intense blue of angel's robe, right-hand side; dark foliage in foreground; (hart panel): dark foliage in foreground; (heraldic panel): red glaze background to lions on arms.

57. For the differing uses of oil and egg as a binding medium see Dunkerton 1991, pp.188ff.

58. Green earth in underpaint layers for the flesh paint was identified microscopically and by EDX analysis. The fine blue-green pigment particles were shown to contain potassium, aluminium, silicon and iron. No copper was detected in the samples.

59. This is contrary to those who believed the exterior was painted separately (e.g. Evans, *Archaeological Journal*, 1950, p.4).

60. The manufactured pigment lead-tin yellow is known in two distinct varieties termed 'type I' and 'type II'. The pigment identified in the Wilton Diptych is the earlier and rarer form called 'type II', and has an origin in the technology of coloured glass making. As well as combined lead and tin oxides, silicon is an essential constituent in this form. Lead-tin yellow 'type II' has a particular connection with Florence in Italian Trecento painting; it has been identified also on an altarpiece in Dijon dated 1396 by Broederlam (M. Comblen-Sonkes and N. Veronée-Verhaegen, *Les Primitifs Flamands: Le Musée des Beaux-Arts de Dijon*, vol. I, Brussels, 1986, p.74). Some further commentary on the identification and history of use of lead-tin yellow can be found in H. Kühn, 'Lead-tin Yellow' in *Artists' Pigments: A Handbook of their History and Characteristics*, vol. II, op. cit. (note 54).

61. The structure and constitution of the foliage greens are remarkably complex. However, small touches of paint representing grey-green foliage in the foregrounds of both the Virgin and Child panel and the hart panel comprise the same layer structure of charcoal black, followed by a mixture of natural orpiment (mineral arsenic trisulphide) and indigo, with a final highlight principally of orpiment. It is unlikely that precisely this technique should be used on both front and reverse if two different painters were involved.

62. For recent technical analysis of Bohemian fourteenth- and fifteenth-century panel painting, see *Technologia Artis*, Yearbook of the Archives of Historical Art Technology, Prague 1992, pp.43–78. For Broederlam see L. Kockaert, 'Note on the Painting Technique of Melchior Broederlam', in Preprint of ICOM Committtee for Conservation, 7th Triennal Meeting, Copenhagen 1984, Section 19, pp.7–9.

63. Barron 1990, pp.132–49. A contemporary illustrated account is the manuscript written by a French chronicler, Jean Creton (London, British Library, Harley MS 1319). See Maunde Thompson, BM, V, 1904, pp.160–72, and 267–70.

64. CPR 1396–9, p.596.

65. See Davies 1957, pp.96ff., and Harvey, *Archaeologia*, 1961, pp.2ff.

66. Gambarini 1731, pp.4 and 61.

The Recent Treatment of the Wilton Diptych

The construction and painting techniques of the diptych have been described in an earlier chapter. They can be summarised as combining Northern European and Italian methods of panel painting to produce an inherently well-made object robust enough to survive the wear and tear of handling and travel. The excellent state of the inside of the diptych and of the hart panel demonstrates its soundness.

There were three reasons for undertaking work on the diptych while it was being examined and recorded for this catalogue. First, no matter how carefully chosen and correctly handled, almost all the materials used in the construction and painting of the two panels are subject to natural deterioration as they age. Secondly and thirdly, accident and human intervention had led to haphazard alterations in the appearance of the diptych.

Natural ageing of the diptych has affected the frame more than the painted surfaces. Much of the gilding on the frame of the exterior has flaked away; the top edge, sides and frame of the interior have also suffered. The main cause of this is probably slight shrinkage of the oak panels. The chalk ground is brittle and is easily loosened by even slight movement of the wood underneath. (The painted parts of the panel, but not the frame, have a mat of parchment fibres beneath the ground, partly intended to minimise the effects of the movement of the wood.) Much of the remaining gilding on the frame has needed consolidation since the diptych came to the Gallery in 1929. The recent examination provided an opportunity to make a minute check of all the gilding and to secure the many partly detached areas with sturgeon's glue. This glue is flexible when dry and can be diluted sufficiently to be introduced through the craquelure of the ground and under the edges left by old losses.

The changes in the painted parts which have occurred naturally (though not intentionally) are described on pp.80–1. The most significant are the fading of Saint Edward's robe and the tarnishing and blackening of the silver leaf of the helm, though the severe accidental damage to the heraldic panel may have contributed to the latter.

Some of the damage is of unknown origin. The loss of the *sgraffito* pattern and underlying gold from the area of Saint Edmund's belt could be due to an accident, as could the loss of the painted outline and detail from the lion's head. Equally, mistreatment during an earlier cleaning might have led to those damages. However, the large loss in the heraldic panel must have been due to an accident. The ground and fibres have been washed away, exposing the oak panel. The most probable cause is a considerable quantity of water dripping onto the panel when it was lying flat, eventually dissolving the rabbit-skin glue (the binding material of the ground) and carrying the ground in liquid form over the surrounding paint and gold, where it settled and dried (Fig. 33).

One of the main objectives of the recent treatment was to increase the legibility of the heraldic panel by removing the ground which had been washed onto its surface. This was the most difficult part because the ground was much thicker and harder than the paint and gold which it covered. The ground could be softened with a damp swab but only at the risk of damaging the very fragile original surface below. Dry removal, using a small scalpel and an operating microscope at up to 15 × magnification, combined with occasional dabbing of the more stubborn areas with a minute damp swab, proved to be the best method.

Turning from accidental damage to human interference, the frame of the front had been re-gilded, probably in the late nineteenth century. The re-gilding may have been done when the diptych was displayed in a framework at Wilton House. All of the frame of the front, except for narrow strips at either side of both panels, was re-gilded using unburnished thick gold leaf over an oil mordant, suggesting that the diptych was displayed with a glazing bar down the centre and bars at either side.

The removal of the new gold was very laborious: the oil mordant (which varied in thickness from about 0.2mm to about 0.8mm) was hard and brittle and could be detached from the original gold underneath by very gentle tapping. Its removal was probably helped by there having been a layer of surface dirt on the frame when the mordant was applied, which prevented it sticking too fiercely. The removal of the new gold revealed the original water gilding to be in good condition, but partly worn away in the lower

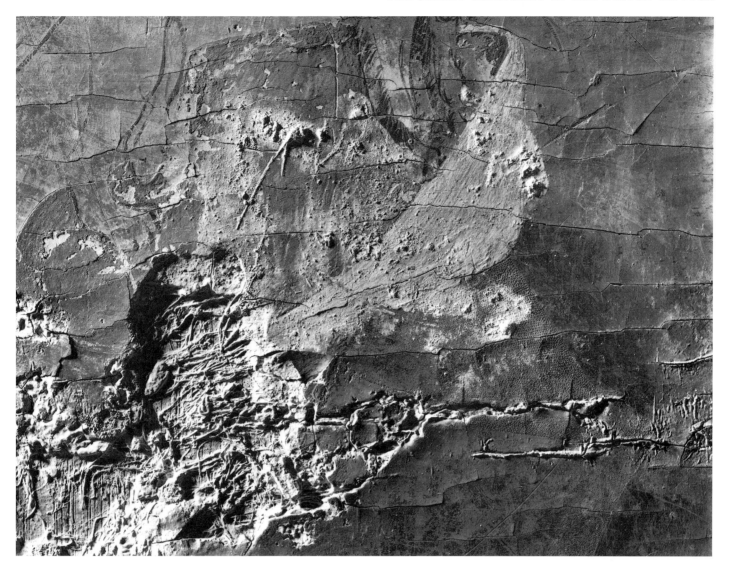

part of the outer edges. This would be the natural place to hold the diptych while opening or closing it; perhaps the gold was worn away by Richard II's own hands.

The final part of the treatment was the removal of surface dirt, yellow varnish and a few re-touchings from the painted surfaces. The re-touchings were in watercolour, not used as a re-touching medium until the second half of the nineteenth century, and may have been contemporary with the re-gilding of the frame. The layer of surface dirt on the reverse was much thicker than that on the inside, perhaps because the inside had been cleaned more recently or because the diptych had been closed for much of its existence. The hart panel was particularly dulled by engrained surface dirt which had made the black landscape lighter and greyer as well as obscuring the delicate tonal modelling of the hart itself.

The removal of the watercolour re-touchings exposed old losses in the landscape to the right of Saint John's leg, an area which was originally intended to be gilded and where the paint had flaked away from the red bole preparation. Several small losses elsewhere on the inside panels had been re-touched. Some of the green underpaint of the flesh exposed by the top layer flaking away had been partially disguised, but not reconstructed, in the earlier restoration, for example the king's hands and the scratches on the face of the kneeling angel.

The paint losses on the front were treated very much as they had been in the earlier restoration. The loss in the landscape, which exposed red bole, was reconstructed, as were small losses elsewhere on both panels. The losses of the top layer of paint in the king's hands and the angels' faces were partially disguised with a warm transparent glaze intended to reduce the startling effect of the green underpaint. The large damage on the heraldic panel was left unrestored, but a number of distracting scratches on the hart panel were re-touched.

Fig. 33 The large damage in the heraldic panel showing the oak with fibres laid across it, where water damage has washed the chalk out of the hole and on to the surrounding paint and gold. Photographed in raking light.

Bibliography

Works cited in abbreviated form in the notes:

Age of Chivalry	*The Age of Chivalry. Art in Plantagenet England 1200–1400*. Exhibition catalogue (eds. J.J.G. Alexander and P. Binski), Royal Academy, London 1987.
BM	*The Burlington Magazine*
CCR	Calendar of the Close Rolls preserved in the Public Record Office, Richard II, vol. VI, AD 1396–1399, London 1927.
CPR	Calendar of the Patent Rolls preserved in the Public Record Office. Richard II, vol. III AD 1385–1389, London 1900, vol. IV AD 1388–1392, London 1902, vol. V AD 1391–1396, London 1905, vol. VI AD 1396–1399, London 1909.
Die Parler	*Die Parler und der schöne Stil 1350–1400. Europäische Kunst unter den Luxemburgen*, Cologne, vols. 1, 2 and 3, 1978, vol. 4 (International Colloquium), 1980, Resultatband 1980.
Essays McKisack	*The Reign of Richard II. Essays in honour of May McKisack* (eds. F.R.H. Du Boulay and C.M. Barron), London 1971.
GBA	*Gazette des Beaux-Arts*
JWCI	*Journal of the Warburg and Courtauld Institutes*
PRO	Public Record Office, London
Westminster Chronicle	*The Westminster Chronicle 1381–94* (eds. L.C. Hector and B.F. Harvey), Oxford 1982.

A comprehensive bibliography on the Wilton Diptych is given by S. Whittingham in *Gazette des Beaux-Arts*, XCVIII, 1981, pp.148–50.

J.J.G. Alexander, 'Painting and Manuscript Illumination for Royal Patrons in the Later Middle Ages', in V. J. Scattergood and J.W. Sherborne (eds.), *English Court Culture in the Later Middle Ages*, London 1983, pp.140–62.

J.J.G. Alexander and M. Kauffmann, *English Illuminated Manuscripts 700–1500* (exhibition catalogue), Bibliothèque Royale Albert 1er, Brussels 1973.

J. Anstis, *Register of the Order of the Garter*, vols. I and II, London 1724.

F. Autrand, *Charles VI*, Paris 1986.

G.E. Aylmer and R. Cant, *A History of York Minster*, Oxford 1977.

C. Barron, 'The Deposition of Richard II', in J. Taylor and W. Childs (eds.), *Politics and Crisis in Fourteenth Century England*, Gloucester 1990, pp.132–49.

M. Bath, 'The White Hart, the Cerf Volant and the Wilton Diptych', in the *Third International Beast, Epic and Fabliau Colloquium*, Munster 1979, pp.25–42 (typescript in the National Gallery archives).

C.R. Beard, 'The Wilton Diptych – English!', in *The Connoisseur*, LXXXVIII, 1931, p.375.

C. Beaune, 'Costume et Pouvoir en France à la fin du Moyen Age', in *Revue des Sciences humaines*, vol. 183, 1981, pp.125–46.

M.J. Bennett, 'The Court of Richard II and the Promotion of Literature', in B. Hanawalt (ed.), *Chaucer's England: Literature in Historical Context*, Minneapolis 1992.

P. Binski, 'What was the Westminster Retable?', in *Journal of the British Archaeological Association*, CXL, 1987, pp.152–74.

W.H. Bliss and J.A. Twemlow, *Calendar of Entries in the Papal Registers relating to Great Britain and Ireland*, IV, 1364–1401, London 1902.

D. Bomford, J. Dunkerton, D. Gordon and A. Roy, *Art in the Making. Italian Painting before 1400* (exhibition catalogue), The National Gallery, London 1989.

T. Borenius, 'Das Wilton Diptychon', in *Pantheon*, XVII, July 1936, pp.209–14.

T. Borenius and E.W. Tristram, *English Medieval Painting*, Florence 1927, reprinted New York 1976.

J.D. d'A. Boulton, *The Knights of the Crown. The Monarchical Orders of Knighthood in Later Medieval Europe 1325–1520*, Woodbridge 1987.

G. Brière, 'Un nouveau primitif français au Musée du Louvre', in *Gazette des Beaux-Arts*, 1919, pp.233–44.

J. Cherry, 'The Dunstable Swan Jewel', in *The Journal of the British Archaeological Association*, XXXII, 1969, pp.38–53.

M.V. Clarke 'The Wilton Diptych', in *The Burlington Magazine*, LVIII, 1931, pp.283–94. Reprinted in L.S. Sutherland and M. McKisack (eds.), *Fourteenth Century Studies*, Oxford 1937.

K.H. Clasen, *Der Meister der Schönen Madonnen – Herkunft, Entfaltung und Umkreis*, Berlin and New York 1974.

J.S. Cotman, *Engravings of Sepulchral Brasses in Norfolk and Suffolk*, vol. I, *Sepulchral Brasses of the County of Norfolk*, London 1839.

W.G. Constable, 'The Date and Nationality of the Wilton Diptych', in *The Burlington Magazine*, 55, 1929, pp.36–45.

Sir M. Conway, 'The Wilton Diptych', in *The Burlington Magazine*, 55, 1929, pp.209–12.

G.W. Coopland, *Philippe de Mézières. Letter to Richard II*, Liverpool 1975.

F.H. Cripps-Day, 'The Wilton Diptych – English!', in *The Connoisseur*, XCI, 1933, pp.167–9.

H.S. Cronin (ed.), *Rogeri Dymok. Liber contra XII Errores et Hereses Lollardorum*, London 1921.

L. Cust, 'Portraits of Richard II', in *Exhibition Illustrative of Early English Portraiture*, Burlington Fine Arts Club, London 1909, pp.16–22.

M. Davies, *National Gallery Catalogues. French School*, 2nd ed., London 1957.

M. Day and R. Steele (eds.), 'Mum and the Sothsegger', in *Early English Text Society*, series no.199, London 1936.

C. Dehaisnes, *Documents et extraits divers concernant l'histoire de l'art, dans la Flandre, L'Artois et le Hainaut avant le XVe siècle*, Lille 1886.

F. Devon, *Issues of the Exchequer*, London 1837.

E. Dostal, *Contributions to the History of the Czech Art of Illumination about the year 1400*, Brno 1928.

L. Douët d'Arcq, *Choix de pièces relatives au règne de Charles VI*, Société de l'histoire de France, Paris 1864.

L. Duls, *Richard II in the Early Chronicles*, Mouton/The Hague/Paris 1975.

J. Dunkerton, S. Foister, D. Gordon and N. Penny, *Giotto to Dürer. Early Renaissance Painting in the National Gallery*, London 1991.

P. Eames, *Furniture in England, France and the Netherlands from the Twelfth to the Fifteenth Century*, London 1977.

J. Evans, 'The Wilton Diptych Reconsidered', in *Archaeological Journal*, CV, for the year 1948, published 1950, pp.1–5.

Froissart (ed. K. de Lettenhove), *Oeuvres de Froissart. Chroniques*, Brussels, IX, 1869, XIV and XVI, 1872.

R.M. Fry, 'On a Fourteenth Century Sketchbook', in *The Burlington Magazine*, X, 1906–7, pp.31–8.

R.M. Fry (ed. D. Sutton), *Letters*, London 1972.

V.H. Galbraith, 'A new life of Richard II', in *History*, March 1942, pp.223ff. (review of Anthony Steel, *Richard II*, Cambridge 1941).

V.H. Galbraith (ed.), *The Anonimalle Chronicle 1333 to 1381*, Manchester 1927.

M. Galway, 'The Wilton Diptych: A Postscript', in *The Archaeological Journal*, 107, for the year 1950, published 1952, pp.9–14.

C. Gaspar and F. Lyna, *Les Principaux Manuscrits à Peintures de la Bibliothèque Royale de Belgique*, I, Paris 1937.

C. Gambarini, *Description of the Earl of Pembroke's Pictures*, 1731.

A. Goodman, *John of Gaunt: the Exercise of Princely Power in Fourteenth-Century Europe*, London 1992.

C. Given-Wilson, *The Royal Household and the King's Affinity: Service Politics and Finance in England 1360–1413*, London 1986.

D. Gordon, 'A new discovery in the Wilton Diptych', in *The Burlington Magazine*, CXXXIV, 1992, pp.662–7.

F.M. Graves (ed.), *Deux Inventaires de la maison d'Orléans (1389 et 1408)*, Paris 1926.

R.F. Green, 'King Richard II's books revisited', in *The Library*, XXXI, 1976, pp.235–9.

R.F. Green, *Poets and Princepleasers: Literature and the English Court in the Late Middle Ages*, Toronto 1980.

R. Griffin, 'The Arms of Richard II as shown in windows at Westwell and Wateringbury', in *Archaeologia Cantiana*, XIV, ii, 1935, pp.170ff.

J. Guiffrey, 'Inventaire des Tapisseries du Roi Charles VI vendues par les anglais en 1422', in *Bibliothèque de l'Ecole des Chartes*, XLVIII, 1887, pp.59–110 and 396–444.

B. Hanawalt (ed.), *Chaucer's England: Literature in Historical Context*, Minneapolis 1992.

J.H. Harvey, 'Some London Painters of the 14th and 15th Centuries', in *The Burlington Magazine*, LXXXIX, 1947, pp.303–5.

J.H. Harvey, *Gothic England. A Survey of National Culture 1300–1550*, 2nd ed., Batsford 1948.

J.H. Harvey, 'The Wilton Diptych', letter in *The Month*, 2, December 1949, pp.433–5.

J.H. Harvey, 'The Wilton Diptych – A Re-examination', in *Archaeologia*, 98, Oxford 1961, pp.1–24.

J.H. Harvey, 'Richard II and York', in F.R.H. Du Boulay and C. M Barron (eds.), *The Reign of Richard II*, London 1971.

J.H. Harvey and D.G. King, 'Winchester College Stained Glass', in *Archaeologia*, 103, 1971, pp.149–77.

L.C. Hector and B.F. Harvey (eds. and trans.), *The Westminster Chronicle, 1381–94*, Oxford 1982.

P. Helyot, *Histoire des ordres monastiques*, VIII, Paris 1719.

J.A. Herbert, *The Sherborne Missal*, Oxford 1920.

H. Hlavackova, 'La Madone de Most. Imitation et Symbole', in *Revue de l'Art*, 1985, pp.59–65.

G. Kipling 'Richard II's "Sumptuous Pageants" and the Idea of Civic Triumph', in D.M. Bergeron (ed.), *Pageantry in the Shakespearean Theater*, Athens, Georgia, 1985.

C.L. Kingsford, 'Our Lady of the Pew – The King's Oratory or Closet in the Palace of Westminster', in *Archaeologia*, 68, 1917, pp.1–20.

E.W. Kirsch, *Five Illuminated Manuscripts of Giangaleazzo Visconti*, University Park and London 1991.

C.L. Kuhn, 'Herman Scheere and English Illumination of the Early Fifteenth Century', in *Art Bulletin*, 1940, pp.138–56.

P.A. Lemoisne, *Gothic Painting in France. Fourteenth and Fifteenth Centuries*, Florence and Paris 1931.

W.R. Lethaby, 'London and Westminster Painters in the Middle Ages', in *The Walpole Society*, I, 1911–12, pp.69–72.

M. Levi d'Ancona, *The Garden of the Renaissance. Botanical Symbolism in Italian Painting*, Florence 1977.

R. Lightbown, *Medieval European Jewellery*, Victoria and Albert Museum, London 1992.

M. McKisack, *The Fourteenth Century, 1307–1399*, Oxford 1959, reprinted 1991.

G. Mathew, *The Court of Richard II*, London 1968.

Sir E. Maunde Thompson 'A Contemporary Account of the Fall of Richard II', in *The Burlington Magazine*, 5, 1904, pp.160–72 and 267–78.

A. Matajcek and J. Pesina, *Gothic Painting in Bohemia 1350–1450*, 4th ed., Prague 1955.

M. Meiss, *French Painting in the Time of Jean de Berry. The late XIV Century and the Patronage of the Duke*, London and New York 1967.

M. Meiss, *French Painting in the Time of Jean de Berry. The Limbourgs and their Contemporaries*, London and New York 1974.

P. Meyer, 'L'Entrevue d'Ardres. 1396', in *Annuaire-Bulletin de la Société de l'Histoire de France*, XVIII, 1881, pp.209–24.

J.T. Micklethwaite, 'A Description of the Chapel of St Erasmus in Westminster Abbey', in *Archaeologia*, XLIV, 1873, pp.93–9.

L. Mirot, 'Un Trousseau royal à la fin du XIV siècle', in *Mémoires de la Société de l'histoire de Paris et de l'Ile de France*, XXIX, Paris 1902, pp.125–58.

L. Monnas, 'Developments in Figured Velvet Weaving in Italy during the 14th Century', in *Bulletin du Liaison du Centre Internationale d'Etudes de Textiles Anciens*, 1986, I and II, pp.63–100.

T. Müller and E. Steingräber, 'Die Französische Goldemailplastik um 1400', in *Münchner Jahrbuch der Bildenden Kunst*, V, 1954, pp.29–79.

J. Nichols, *A Collection of the Wills of the Kings and Queens of England*, London 1780.

J.G. Nichols, 'On Collars of the Royal Livery', in *The Gentleman's Magazine*, XVII, 1842, pp.157–61; 250–8; 378–9.

J.G. Nichols, 'Observations on the Heraldic Devices discovered on the Effigies of Richard II and his Queen', in *Archaeologia*, XXIX, 1842, pp.32–59.

N.H. Nicolas, 'On the Origin and History of the Badge and Mottoes of Edward Prince of Wales', in *Archaeologia*, XXXI, 1846, pp.350–84.

J.G. Noppen, 'The painter of Richard II', in *The Burlington Magazine*, LX, 1932, pp.82–7.

W. Paley Baildon, 'A Wardrobe Account of 16–17 Richard II.1393–4', in *Archaeologia*, vol. 62, pt.2, 1911, pp.497–514.

F. Palgrave, *The Antient Kalendars and Inventories of the Treasury of His Majesty's Exchequer*, London 1836.

J.J.N. Palmer, 'The Background to Richard's marriage to Isabel of France', in *Bulletin of the Institute of Historical Research*, 1971, pp.1–17.

J.J.N. Palmer, *England, France and Christendom*, London 1972.

E. Panofsky, *Early Netherlandish Painting*, vol. I, Cambridge, Mass., 1953.

J.D. Passavant, *Tour of a German Artist in England*, Eng. trs. by Elizabeth Rigby, later Lady Eastlake, London 1836.

E. Perroy, *The Diplomatic Correspondence of Richard II*, Royal Historical Society, Camden, 3rd series, XLVIII, 1933.

J. Pesina, 'Zur Frage der Chronologie des Schönen Stils in der Tafelmalerei Böhmens', in *Jahrbuch des Kunsthistorischen Institutes der Universität Graz*, 1972–3, Band VII, pp.1–28.

H.J. Plenderleith and H. Maryon, 'The Royal Bronze Effigies in Westminster Abbey', in *The Antiquaries Journal*, XXXIX, 1959, pp.87–90.

A.E. Popham, 'The Wilton Diptych', in *Apollo*, VIII, December 1928, pp. 317–18.

E. Powell, 'A King's Tomb', in *History Today*, October 1965, pp.713–18.

R.B. Rackham, 'The Nave of Westminster', in *Proceedings of the British Academy*, IV, 1909–10, pp.35–96.

E. Rickert, 'Richard II's books', in *The Library*, 4th series, XIII, 1933, pp.144–7.

M. Rickert, 'Herman the Illuminator', in *The Burlington Magazine*, LXI, 1935, p.39.

M. Rickert, *The Reconstructed Carmelite Missal*, London 1952.

M. Rickert, *Painting in Britain: The Middle Ages*, in The Pelican History of Art, 1st ed., 1954, 2nd ed., Harmondsworth 1965.

M. Rickert, 'The So-Called Beaufort Hours and York Psalter', in *The Burlington Magazine*, CIV, 1962, pp.238–46.

H.T. Riley (ed.), Thomas Walsingham's *Historia Anglicana*, vol. II, *AD 1381–1422*, London 1864.

H.T. Riley, *Memorials of London and London Life in the XIIIth, XIVth, and XVth Centuries*, London 1868.

P.R. Robinson, *Catalogue of Dated and Datable Manuscripts c.733–1600 in Cambridge Libraries*, Cambridge 1988.

Royal Commission on Historical Monuments, London, vol. I, *Westminster Abbey*, London 1924.

W.H. St John Hope, 'On the Funeral Effigies of the Kings and Queens of England with special reference to Westminster Abbey', in *Archaeologia*, 60, 1907, pp.517–70.

L.F. Sandler, *Gothic Manuscripts 1285–1385. A Survey of Manuscripts Illuminated in the British Isles*, vol. V, London and Oxford 1986.

N. Saul, 'Richard II and Westminster Abbey', in *The Monasteries and Lay Society*, Oxford 1994 (in press).

V.J. Scattergood and J.W. Sherborne (eds.), *English Court Culture in the Late Middle Ages*, London 1983.

G. Scharf, *Description of the Wilton House Diptych*, Arundel Society, London 1882.

K. Scott, *Later Gothic Manuscripts 1390–1490. A Survey of Manuscripts Illuminated in the British Isles*, vol. VI, London 1994 (in press).

W.A. Shaw, 'The Early English School of Portraiture', in *The Burlington Magazine*, LXV, 1934, pp.171–84.

A. Simpson, *The Connections between English and Bohemian Painting during the Second Half of the Fourteenth Century*, PhD thesis, Courtauld Institute of Art, London 1978, published 1984.

A. Simpson, 'English Art during the Second Half of the Fourteenth Century' in *Die Parler*, Resultatband, 1980, pp.137–59.

B. Spencer, *Pilgrim Souvenirs and Secular Badges. Salisbury Museum Medieval Catalogue*, Part 2, Salisbury 1990.

A.P. Stanley, *Historical Memorials of Westminster Abbey*, London 1869.

A.P. Stanley, 'On an examination of the Tombs of Richard II and Henry III', in *Archaeologia*, 45, 1880, pp.309–25.

A. Steel, *Richard II*, Cambridge 1941.

C. Sterling, *Les Peintres du Moyen Age*, Paris 1942.

C. Sterling, *La Peinture Médiévale à Paris 1300-1500*, Paris 1987.

G.B. Stow (ed.), *Historia Vitae et Regni Ricardi Secundi*, University of Pennsylvania Press, 1977.

P. Strohm, *Social Chaucer*, London 1989.

K.M. Swoboda (ed.), *Gotik in Böhmen*, Munich 1969.

L.E Tanner, *Unknown Westminster Abbey*, Harmondsworth 1948.

L.E. Tanner, 'Some representations of St Edward in Westminster Abbey and elsewhere', in *Journal of the British Archaeological Association*, 3rd series, XV, 1952, pp.1–12.

J. Taylor, 'Richard II's Views on Kingship', in *Proceedings of the Leeds Philosophical and Literary Society, Literary and Historical Section*, vol. XIV, Part V, 1971, pp.189–205.

H. Thurston, 'The Wilton Diptych', in *The Month*, CLIV, 2, July 1929, pp.27–37.

T.F. Tout, *Chapters in the Administrative History of Medieval England*, Manchester, IV, 1928; V, 1930.

E.W. Tristram: 'The Wilton Diptych', in *The Month*, 1949, I, pp.379–90; II, pp.18–36 and 433–5; III, 1950, pp.234–8.

E. W. Tristram, *English Wall Painting of the Fourteenth Century*, London 1955.

A. Tuck, *Richard II and the English Nobility*, London 1973.

D.H. Turner, 'The Bedford Hours and Psalter', in *Apollo*, LXXVI, 1962, pp.265–70.

R. Twysden (ed.), *Chronica W. Thorn mon. S. Augustini Cantuariae* in *Historia Anglicana Scriptores*, X, 1652.

C. Tyerman, *England and the Crusades 1095–1588*, Chicago and London 1988.

G. Waagen, *Treasures of Art at Great Britain*, III, London 1854, pp.150–1.

G. Waagen, *A Walk through the Art Treasures Exhibition in Manchester*, London 1857.

M.E. Walcott, 'The Inventories of Westminster Abbey at the Dissolution', in *Transactions of the London and Middlesex Archaeological Society*, IV, iii, for the year 1873, published 1875, pp.313–76.

H.F. Westlake, *Westminster Abbey*, vol. II, London 1923.

J. Wickham Legg, 'On an inventory of the Vestry in Westminster Abbey taken in 1388', in *Archaeologia*, LII, for the year 1889, published 1890, pp.195–286.

J. Wickham Legg, *English Coronation Records*, London 1901.

S. Whittingham, 'The chronology of the Portraits of Richard II', in *The Burlington Magazine*, CXIII, 1971, pp.12–21.

S. Whittingham, 'The Date of the Wilton Diptych', in *Gazette des-Beaux Arts*, XCVIII, 1981, pp.145–50.

E. Wilkins, *The Rose-Garden Game. The Symbolic Background to European Prayer Beads*, London 1969.

F. Wormald, 'The Wilton Diptych', in *Journal of the Warburg and Courtauld Institutes*, XVII, 1954, pp.191–203.

S. Wright, 'The Author Portraits in the Bedford Psalter and Hours: Gower, Chaucer and Hoccleve', in *British Library Journal*, vol. 18, no.2, 1992, pp.190–201.

T. Wright (ed.), *Political Poems and Songs relating to English History*, vol. 1. *Rerum Britannicarum Medii Aevi Scriptores*, London 1859.

J.H. Wylie, *A History of England under Henry IV*, 1, 1399–1404, London 1884; IV, 1411–1413, 1898.

GLOSSARY OF HERALDIC TERMS

Badge a device or emblem usually worn as a mark of identification, ownership or allegiance

Cap of maintenance a cap of dignity borne by a person of noble rank

Couchant descriptive of animals lying down

Cross patonce a cross with three splayed points at the end of each arm

England and France ancient the royal arms as used from 1340 to *c.*1406 consisting of the arms of the Kingdom of France (azure semé with fleurs-de-lis) quartered with those of the Kingdom of England (gules three lions passant guardant or)

England and France modern the royal arms as used from *c.*1406 to 1603. Around 1406 the fleurs-de-lis in the quartering of the French arms described above were reduced to three

Gorged wearing a collar around the neck

Guardant descriptive of a beast with its head turned towards the observer

Gules red

Impaled two coats of arms combined side by side on a shield

Lodged descriptive of a beast of the chase lying down

Martlet a martin or swallow without feet used as a bearing

Or gold

Passant descriptive of animals walking

Semé scattered with

LENDERS TO THE EXHIBITION

Cambridge, The Master and Fellows of St John's College (No. 2)
Cambridge, The Master, Fellows and Scholars of Trinity Hall (No. 15)
Hastingwood, Essex, J.F.W. Auld (No. 17)
London, The British Library (Nos. 5, 6, 9, 10, 19, 41 and 42)
London, The Trustees of the British Museum (Nos. 11, 12, 14 and 16)
London, The Museum of London (Nos. 20, 24–8, 31, 33–40)
London, The Dean and Chapter of Westminster (Nos. 3 and 4)
Lyons, Musée des Tissus Historiques, (No. 18)
Trustees of the Ninth Duke of Northumberland's Will (No. 8)
Oxford, The President and Fellows of Corpus Christi College (No. 7)
Prague, Národní Galerie (No. 32)
Private Collection (No. 29)
Salisbury and South Wiltshire Museum (Nos. 21 and 22)
Shrewsbury Museums (No. 1)
Troyes, Musée des Beaux-Arts et d'Archéologie de Troyes (No. 13)
Winchester, The Warden and Scholars of Winchester College (No. 30)

LIST OF WORKS IN THE EXHIBITION

1. *Charter of Richard II to Shrewsbury*
   1389
   Vellum, 69.5 × 100.5 cm
   Shrewsbury Museums (Muniments 1.24)
   Fig. 4

2. *Book of Statutes (Statuta Angliae)*
   1388–99
   Vellum, 34.3 × 24 cm
   Cambridge, St John's College (MS A 7)
   Fig. 3

3. *Richard II Enthroned*
   *c.*1395(?)
   Panel, 213.5 × 110 cm
   London, Westminster Abbey
   Plate 26

4. The *Liber Regalis* (Book of the Coronation Order)
   *c.*1390–9
   Vellum, 27.3 × 17.2 cm
   London, Westminster Abbey (MS 38)
   Plate 25

5. *Libellus geomancie* (Book of Astrological Tables written
   for Richard II)
   1390–1
   Vellum, 22.5 × 15.5 cm
   London, British Library (Royal MS 12 C.V.)

6. *Book of Hours and Psalter*
   *c.*1380–90
   Vellum, 27 × 19 cm
   London, British Library (Additional MS 16968)

7. *The Lapworth Missal*
   1398
   Vellum, 44.5 × 27.5 cm
   Oxford, Corpus Christi College (MS 394)

8. *The Sherborne Missal*
   Between 1395 and 1407
   Vellum, 53.3 × 38.1 cm
   Illuminated by John Siferwas
   The Trustees of the Will of the Ninth Duke of
   Northumberland (currently British Library MS
   loan 82)
   Plate 29

9. *Book of Offices and Prayers*
Beginning of the 15th century
Vellum, 23 × 16 cm
Signed by Herman Scheerre on f.37
Inscribed 'Omnia levia sunt amanti' on f.67
London, British Library (Additional MS 16998)

10. *Book of Hours* (The Beaufort Hours)
Beginning of the 15th century
Vellum, 22 × 15 cm
Inscribed 'Omnia levia sunt amanti/ si quis amat non laborat' and 'de daer' on f.23v
London, British Library (Royal MS 2.A. XVIII)
Plate 30

11. *Jug* (The Ashanti Ewer)
1377–99
Copper alloy, height 40.2 cm
Known as the 'Ashanti Ewer' because it was found in the palace of Ashanti, West Africa, in the 19th century
London, British Museum (MLA 96, 7–27, 1)
Fig. 8

12. *The Dunstable Swan Jewel*
c.1400
Gold with white and black enamel, 3.2 × 2.5 cm
Found at the Dominican friary at Dunstable
London, British Museum (MLA, 1966, 7–3, 1)
Plate 9

13. *Badge of the White Hart*
c.1377–99
Copper alloy, silver and enamel, gilt, diameter 3.5 cm
Troyes, Musée des Beaux-Arts (871.6.1)
Plate 10

14. *Horary Quadrant*
Inscribed 1399
Brass, originally gilded, length 8.9 cm
London, British Museum (MLA 60, 5–19, 1)
Fig. 11

15. Roger Dymok's *Liber contra XII Errores et Hereses Lollardorum* (Treatise against the 12 errors and heresies of the Lollards)
c.1395
Vellum, 26.3 × 18.7 cm
Cambridge, Trinity Hall (MS 17)
Plate 11

16. *Livery Badge of a White Hart, lodged with crown collar and chain*
c.1390–9
Pewter, 3.7 × 4 cm
London, British Museum (1856, 6–27, 117)
Fig. 10

17. *Livery Badge of a White Hart, lodged with crown collar and chain*
c.1390–9
Pewter, 3.6 × 3.3 cm
J.F.W. Auld (currently on loan to the Museum of London)

18. *Chasuble from the reign of Charles VI of France*
c.1400
Polychrome velvet, brocaded with gold, woven with broomcods and Belts of Espérance, 118 × 52 cm
Lyons, Musée des Tissus Historiques (25688)
Plate 13

19. *Collected Works of Christine de Pisan*
c.1405–10
Vellum, 36.4 × 26.5 cm
London, British Library (Harley MS 4431, vol. II)
Plate 12

20. *Livery Badge of a Broompod*
Late 14th/early 15th century
Pewter, 6.2 × 1.3 cm
Museum of London (8878)

21. *Livery Badge of a Broompod*
Late 14th/early 15th century
Pewter, 6.4 × 1.3 cm
Salisbury and South Wiltshire Museum (61/1990)
Fig. 13

22. *Pilgrim Badge: Saint Edmund*
Early 15th century
Pewter, 5.7 × 1.5 cm
Salisbury and South Wiltshire Museum (205a/1987)
Fig. 14

23. *Brass rubbing of the sepulchral monument to Sir Simon Felbrigg and his wife, Felbrigg Church, Norfolk*
1416
Made by Mrs Christina Reast (see Fig. 15 for 19th-century engraving)

24. *Pilgrim Badge: Crown of Edward the Confessor*
Late 14th/early 15th century
Pewter, 5.8 × 4.8 cm
Museum of London (A24766/28)

25. *Pilgrim Badge: Crown of Edward the Confessor*
Late 14th/early 15th century
Pewter, 2.6 × 2 cm
Museum of London (78/84/10)

26. *Pilgrim Badge: Crown of Edward the Confessor*
Late 14th/early 15th century
Pewter, 2.9 × 2.4 cm
Museum of London (8880)

27. *Pilgrim Badge: Crowned head of Edward the Confessor*
(within circular frame)
Late 14th century
Pewter, 2.4 × 2.2 cm
Museum of London (A2520)

28. *Ampulla of Edward the Confessor: Edward the Confessor*
enthroned on one side, Saint Peter enthroned on the other
Late 13th century
Lead, 9.9 × 5.4 cm
Museum of London (81.475)

29. *Edward the Confessor with the Pilgrim*
*c.*1370
Panel, 77.5 × 73.5 cm
Private Collection

30. *Richard II kneeling before Saint John the Baptist*
*c.*1393
Stained glass, 103 × 65.5 cm
The fragmentary inscription originally read
RICARDUS SECUNDUS REX / ANGLIE ET FRANCIE
(Richard the Second. King of England and France)
Winchester College
Plate 16

31. *Pilgrim Badge: Saint John the Baptist*
14th century
Pewter, 4.5 × 2.8 cm
Museum of London (86.343/2)
Fig. 25

32. *The Virgin and Child*
*c.*1390–1400
Artificial cast stone, height 116.5 cm
Prague, Národní Galerie (P 226)
Fig. 24

33. *Pilgrim Badge: The Virgin and Child*
15th century
Pewter, 3.6 × 1.5 cm
Museum of London (86.202/28)

34. *Pilgrim Badge: The Virgin and Child*
15th century
Pewter, 3.4 × 1.3 cm
Museum of London (86.202/29)

35. *Pilgrim Badge: The Virgin and Child*
14th/15th century
Pewter, 4.5 × 1.7 cm
Museum of London (86.202/35)

36. *Pilgrim Badge: The Virgin and Child*
14th/15th century
Pewter, 3.8 × 1.6 cm
Museum of London (A14613)

37. *Pilgrim Badge: The Virgin and Child*
14th century
Pewter, 6.1 × 2.4 cm
Museum of London (A20828)

38. *Pilgrim Badge: The Virgin and Child*
15th century
Pewter, 3.2 × 2.5 cm
Museum of London (82.255/11)

39. *Pilgrim Badge: The Virgin and Child*
Late 15th century
Copper alloy, 2.8 × 2.8 cm
Museum of London (85.253/1)

40. *Pilgrim Badge: The Virgin and Child*
Late 15th century
Copper alloy, 4.2 × 2.3 cm
Museum of London (80.413)

41. *Epître de Philippe de Mézières*
*c.*1395
Vellum, 25 × 17.8 cm
London, British Library (Royal MS 20. B. VI)
Plate 17

42. *Histoire du Roy d'Angleterre* (History of Richard King
of England) by Jean Creton
Mid-15th century
Vellum, 28.7 × 20.5 cm
London, British Library (Harley MS 1319)
Fig. 32

PICTURE CREDITS